1990
MIZ AMERICA

Les Misérables

This edition published in 2018 by Carlton Books Limited

A division of the Carlton Publishing Group, 20 Mortimer Street
London, W1T 3JW

Printed in Dubai

A CIP catalogue for this book is available from the British Library

ISBN: 978 1 78739 140 6

Much of the material in this book previously appeared in
Les Misérables: From Stage to Screen, 2012.

THE MUSICAL PHENOMENON

Les Misérables

FROM PAGE TO STAGE TO SCREEN

The Ongoing Story of the World's Longest Running Musical

Benedict Nightingale

Martyn Palmer & Matt Wolf

Foreword by
Cameron Mackintosh

Dramatis Personae

The following descriptions have been taken from Victor Hugo's original novel.

Jean Valjean – Hatred was his only weapon, and he resolved to sharpen it in prison and carry it with him when he left. Jean Valjean wept for a long time … And as he wept a new day dawned in his spirit, a day both wonderful and terrible. For some time he had been apprehensively watching this growing radiance of Cosette's beauty, a bright dawn to others but to himself a dawn of ill-omen.

Inspector Javert – His eyes were cold and piercing. His duties were his religion … Javert's mental attitude was made up of two simple principles – respect for authority and hatred of revolt against it.

Fantine – She was beautiful … a beautiful blonde with fine teeth. When Fantine found that she could make ends meet she had a moment of rejoicing. To be able to live by honest toil was like a blessing from heaven.

Cosette (eight years old) – She was thin and pale. Her big eyes in their shadowed sockets seemed almost extinguished by the many tears they had shed.

Cosette (as a young woman) – She was beautiful as well as pretty … Her figure had filled out, her skin was finer, her hair more lustrous and there was a new splendour in her blue eyes.

Marius Pontmercy – Marius … was a handsome young man with thick, very dark hair, a high intelligent forehead, wide, sensitive nostrils, a frank, composed bearing and an expression that was … thoughtful.

Monsieur Thénardier – Thénardier was a small, skinny, sallow-faced man … He smiled constantly as a matter of precaution.

Madame Thénardier – Tall, fair-haired, red-faced, fleshy, broad-shouldered, huge and active … Everything trembled at the sound of her voice, window-panes, furniture, people. They were an ugly and dreadful pair, the Thénardiers, a marriage of cunning and fury.

Eponine (as a young woman) – She was a lean and delicate-looking creature … in other circumstances … her uninhibited gaiety might have made of her something sweet and charming.

The Bishop of Digne – His whole being seemed to radiate happiness. "Love one another." To him everything was contained in those words.
Gavroche – He had no shelter, no food, no fire, no love, but he was light-hearted because he was free.

Friends of the ABC

Enjolras – He had one passion only, justice: one thought only, to remove all obstacles. His speech was roughly inspired and had the tremor of a hymn.
Grantaire – Took great care not to believe anything. A great drinker … he was particularly ugly; but Grantaire's self-esteem was not disconcerted. He stared tenderly at every woman.
Combeferre – His desire was to instill into all minds the broad principles of general ideas; his motto was "Revolution, but civilization".
Feuilly – Feuilly was a fan-maker, an orphan, who had one thought only, to deliver the world from its bonds.
Courfeyrac – Courfeyrac did have that youthful animation that we might call a diabolic beauty of mind … a splendid fellow.
Joly – A hypochondriac. What he had learned from medicine was to be a patient rather than a physician … young, finicky, sickly, joyful … an eccentric agreeable person.
Lesgles – The bald member of the club … His speciality was to succeed at nothing. On the other hand he laughed at everything.
Jean Prouvaire – Addicted to love … his voice was usually delicate, but at times suddenly masculine. He was well read, to the point of erudition. Above all, he was good.

Members of Thénardier's Gang

Montparnasse – A mournful sight, that was Montparnasse. The digestion of what was bad gave him an appetite for what was worse.
Claquesous – He was night … Restless, roving, terrible. He disappeared as if he melted into thin air.
Babet – Babet … thin and shrewd. Transparent but impenetrable. You could see daylight through his bones, but nothing through his eye.
Brujon – A sprightly young fellow, very cunning and clever, with a flurried plaintive look. Dazed by prison … He was sometimes seen for hours … staring … or trembling.

Other Significant Characters

Fauchelevant – A professional man … compelled to earn his living as a carter … [he] had fallen under his cart … [Valjean] got the old man a job as a gardener at a convent.
Bamatabois – The provincial dandy … tormenting a creature … [with] some remark he thought witty and pleasant as, "My, but you're ugly!".
Champmathieu – An unknown wretched being gradually bending beneath the weight of a terrible similarity [to Jean Valjean].

Above: Andreane Neofitou's original costume designs.
Following page: "Lovely Ladies", UK Tour, Cardiff, 2010.

Contents

A Dream Beyond All Dreams

I'm sure the one thing Victor Hugo did not think he had written was a fairy tale. Yet that is what the fabled author, of arguably the greatest social novel ever written, has spawned with the musical *Les Misérables*.

On that fateful day 4 February 1983, when Alain, Claude-Michel and I first met in Paris we may have had dreams of putting on a rewritten version of their show successfully in London but what has happened to the People's musical since it opened in London in October 1985 is a Dream beyond all Dreams. It has touched and changed the lives of myself, the authors, our creative teams, actors and audiences alike all over the world in whatever language it has been acted and sung.

I am often asked what it is that makes audiences and actors so passionate about the material of *Les Mis*, as the show is fondly known. The abbreviation of the title is maybe a clue. In Hugo's story the characters are so personal, so timeless, so universal, they remain a contemporary mirror of ourselves and, despite its seemingly foreboding title *Les Misérables* is our friend and companion. Audiences feel possessive of this timeless tale, where the downtrodden must fight to be heard and sometimes die to be free. Yet in their darkest moments of struggle they find love, life and laughter, and mankind's most redeeming trait, the unquenchable survival of the human spirit.

The French and British connections to *Les Misérables* have always been intertwined. Though this epic tale was born in a country renowned for its Republic and its philosophy, it was written on British soil, in Guernsey where Hugo was in exile. It was raised to musical life through the marriage of a thrilling French score and the power of the English language, (thanks to Herbert Kretzmer's unforgettable words) combined with British stage craft at its finest.

Ironically the idea of turning this classic novel into a musical was inspired by Britain's 19th Century literary counterpart to Hugo, Charles Dickens. Dickens' hugely entertaining and timelessly appealing story *Oliver Twist* about an orphan child being reunited with his grandfather, having survived the trials and tribulations of Victorian poverty and crime, inspired an English cockney, the song writer Lionel Bart, to write another smash hit worldwide musical success *Oliver!* I, catalyst that I am, happened to have produced a revival of the musical that Alain Boublil went to see in January 1978, (almost exactly five years before we were to meet in Paris). It was that performance of *Oliver!* that gave Alain the idea to write a musical of *Les Misérables* which Claude-Michel immediately embraced. I had no inkling of all this until several years into the run of *Les Mis* when by chance I asked Alain how it had all come about and he told me - now if that isn't a fairy tale then I don't know what is.

Above: Cameron Mackintosh on the set of *Les Misérables*, 1987.

But fairy tales have to come to life and no show could have had better dramatic guidance and brilliant stagecraft than *Les Mis* in the hands of the extraordinary directing duo of Trevor Nunn and John Caird. In collaboration with the brilliant design team of John Napier, Andreane Neofitou and David Hersey, their talent and imagination propelled the original production around the world during its first 25 record-breaking years. To mark this great milestone I decided not only to stage a 25th Anniversary concert at the O2 in London, but also to create a new production of this unique musical for another generation. I put together a new duo of directors, Laurence Connor and James Powell, who went back to the drawing board and gave this phenomenal musical a thrilling new staging, with designs based on Victor Hugo's own paintings, brought to life by another brilliant team of designers Matt Kinley, Paule Constable, Christine Rowland and Andreane Neofitou. No musical can exist without the essential combined inspiration of the musical team that work with a composer to bring his work to theatrical life. Every version of this unique musical has relied on the combined talents of John Cameron, Stephen Metcalfe, Stephen Brooker and Chris Jahnke as orchestrators and sound designers Andrew Bruce and Mick Potter. The worldwide success of this new version also inspired Working Title Films, Universal Pictures and the outstanding British film director, Tom Hooper, to take up the challenge of turning the World's longest running stage musical into a daringly different cinematic experience.

This book hopes to share with the reader the ongoing 40-year old rollercoaster journey of Boublil and Schonberg's musical masterpiece - from concept album, to stage, to screen and an equally successful new production - still continuing to break records in its 4th decade; something that has never happened in the history of musical theatre with any other show. When *Les Misérables* premiered in October 1985 Edward Behr, then Arts Editor and critic for *Newsweek* stuck his neck out against the tide of negativity surrounding the opening of the show at the Royal Shakespeare's Barbican Theatre by declaring that *Les Mis* was "a musical that makes history, not just because it hits the jackpot but because, like *West Side Story* it adds to the artistic dimensions of theatre - a believable, universally relevant tale provoking laughter, tears - and the uplift of truly great theatre." He certainly was proved right. Though most of the critics were very negative in their reactions to *Les Mis* at the start - the public weren't. They embraced it immediately, ignored the reviews and voting with their feet literally stormed the box office, to the extent that our opening slogan at London's Palace Theatre, where we transferred, was "Fight to get a ticket!"

Above all, this story, which like every good fairy tale has had such a happy outcome, is a thank you to the public who generation after generation have joined in our Crusade and ensured that Tomorrow Will Always Come. To be continued ...

Cameron Mackintosh, May 2018

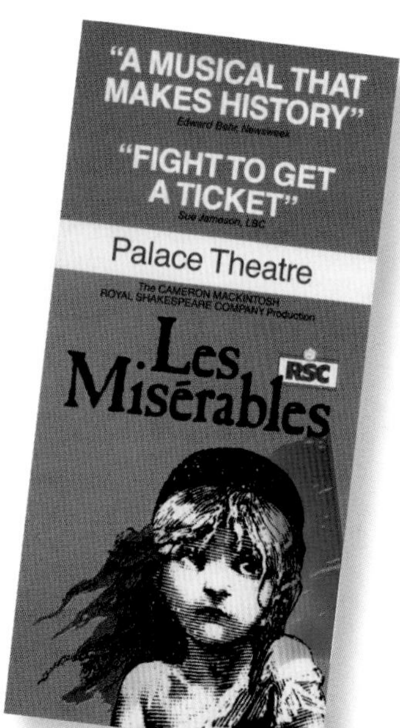

Left: Leaflet featuring the "Fight to get a ticket" slogan, Palace Theatre, 1985.

Below: Hugh Jackman as Jean Valjean rescues Isabelle Allen as Little Cosette from her life of misery in the film of *Les Misérables*.

Bottom: *Town at Dusk* (pen, ink and watercolour on paper) by Victor Hugo, chosen as the front cloth for the *Les Misérables* 25th anniversary production, 2010.

CHAPTER 1

The Origins

"We're doing a musical show … and it's got 'Misérables' in the title. It's got 29 onstage deaths … It's largely about French history … there are no dance routines, no tap shoes, no sequins, no fishnets, no staircase, no big stars, no cowboys, no chimney sweeps, no witches, no wizards. Moreover, there's virtually no advance at the box-office and it's received thumbs-down reviews. How can it possibly succeed?"

That, slightly edited, is what Trevor Nunn said when he came onstage at London's Queen's Theatre on 7 October 2006 to celebrate an occasion that had definitively disproved every rule of musical theatre. Against all the odds, the show that the producer Cameron Mackintosh had asked him and John Caird to stage as part of the Royal Shakespeare Company's 1985 season was celebrating its 21st birthday; not only that, Alain Boublil and Claude-Michel Schönberg's *Les Misérables* had become the world's longest running musical and perhaps also its most beloved.

By its 33rd birthday in 2018, it had run up 13,713 performances in the West End alone. Worldwide, over 100 professional companies had given 54,000 performances of the show in 51 countries and 422 cities, often more than once. During that time it had played to over 70 million people, been translated into 22 languages, including Icelandic, Hebrew and Mauritian Creole, and had won more than 160 major awards in countries from America to Hungary, Argentina to Japan.

The seeds of all this were sown in 1973, when Boublil, then a Paris-based music publisher and successful lyricist, saw Andrew Lloyd Webber and

Below: Alain Boublil with Claude-Michel Schönberg photographed on set during rehearsals at the Barbican in London on 23 September 1985.

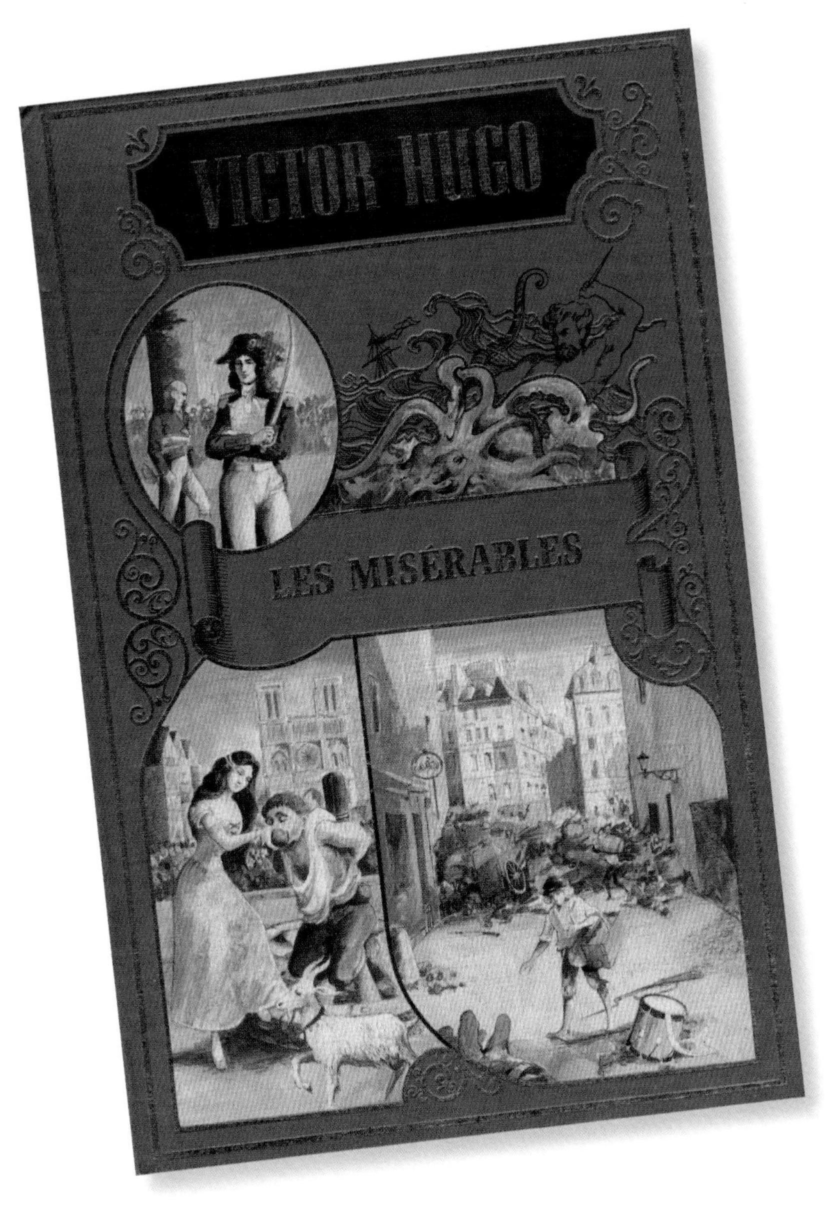

Tim Rice's *Jesus Christ Superstar* on Broadway. After the performance he walked the New York streets until the early hours, excitedly pondering the possibilities of sung-through rock opera. Back in Paris he contacted the record producer, singer and composer with whom he had already started collaborating on pop songs, Claude-Michel Schönberg.

The two men had been friends since they met in 1968, sharing a passion for musicals and opera. Though the Tunis-born Boublil had no

Above: A charming nineteenth-century cover for an edition of Victor Hugo's novel, which was first published in 1862 by Albert Lacroix in Belgium.

Right: An illustration of Jean Valjean by Gustave Brion (1824-77) from the first edition of *Les Misérables*. Brion won numerous medals at the Paris Salon for his paintings and was awarded the Légion d'Honneur in 1863, the year after *Les Misérables* was published.

Left: An original sketch by Victor Hugo of the unloved street urchin Gavroche.

Above: Andreane Neofitou's costume design for factory workers for the original production at the Barbican, London, in 1985.

musical background, and indeed had prepared for a business career at Paris's Institute of Higher Commercial Studies, he had felt the lure of the genre since seeing *West Side Story* as an 18-year-old student in 1959. But Schönberg, himself a distant relative of the pioneering composer Arnold Schönberg and the great-nephew of a *kapelmeister* to Tsar Nicholas II, had been steeped in music from his birth in 1944. His parents, Jewish-Hungarian immigrants, had filled their Brittany house with 78 rpm records: "When I was six or seven I already knew *Carmen*, *Madam Butterfly* and *The Tales of Hoffmann*". Indeed, Schönberg still rates Offenbach, and especially *Hoffmann*, as his major influence.

Helped by the composer Raymond Jeannot and the lyricist Jean-Max Rivière, the two friends created their first show in 1973. *La Révolution Française* was a considerable success, not only as a best-selling record, but also as a series of dramatic tableaux staged in Paris's 4,500-seat Palais des Sports. But what were they to do next?

Then, in January 1978, Boublil saw a London revival of Lionel Bart's *Oliver!* produced by Cameron Mackintosh. That night the French lyricist had a second apotheosis. Dickens's Artful Dodger instantly reminded him of Gavroche, the streetwise urchin in Victor Hugo's *Les Misérables*. And as he watched the British characters, he found himself thinking of their counterparts in the great French novel.

"I was in a kind of trance the whole evening and came out of that incredible theatrical production obsessed," said Boublil. "I was going to do the same. I had no doubts. *Les Misérables* would be our next musical. The characters were all there … So I went back to Paris, spent time with the novel, went through it with my pen thinking this would make a song and this wouldn't, and called Claude-Michel."

So confident and excited were the two men that they did indeed start work, full-time work, giving up their jobs and appalling their friends. Were they mad? Had not even Puccini tried to adapt *Les Misérables*, abandoning the task as too complex? The novel was not only a great classic, it was great in bulk, too. Its 1,200-odd pages are full of incident and of Hugo's lengthy musings.

For Boublil and Schönberg it became a two-year labour of cutting, condensing and shaping.

Subsidiary characters disappeared, and a major decision was made about characters: Thénardier, the innkeeper, was still to be an unscrupulous scoundrel, and Madame Thénardier was to behave as cruelly to Cosette as she does in the novel, but they were also to be comic relief. After all, Thénardier had been played in a major film of *Les Misérables* by Bourvil, a famous French comedian – and Boublil and Schönberg felt a music-theatre audience steeped in the tribulations of Valjean and Fantine should be offered the chance to laugh.

For Schönberg, Boublil is "a man I absolutely trust", and for Boublil, Schönberg is the consummate professional, "always open and, in 40 years of collaboration, never once doing something out of pride or reacting in an egoistic way".

"When we are discussing a scene we have exactly the same vision," said Schönberg. "We speak, speak, speak about the subject. We describe what's happening onstage, what the characters are saying or singing, and from this point I can start writing a few bars of music. I have nothing to prove to him

Left: A view from the sound desk of the stage preparations for the 1980 Paris production.

Below: A first-nigaht ticket to *Les Misérables* at the Palais des Sports in Paris, 1980.

Bottom: A rehearsal pass for the Paris production of *Les Misérables* in 1980.

and he has nothing to prove to me. I can say that a lyric doesn't express what we need, and he can say, 'No, no, I don't feel the music'. And always we go back to the script we're building up. If that's right, the score is usually 90 per cent right." "When we describe a scene," agreed Boublil, "usually the two of us know the kind of music and the kind of words that are needed for it."

Ultimately, Schönberg felt his inspiration was Hugo himself: "the book is a written opera, larger than life, over-the-top, and if you don't reflect that in emphatic music the score cannot work." And, ultimately, Boublil feels his own inspiration was Schönberg's interpretation of Hugo: "There is a never-ending symbiosis between us, but I couldn't go on to write a lyric without hearing Claude-Michel's music."

Consistently enough, the original ideas for numbers sometimes came directly from Hugo's own words, sometimes from the collaborators' memories or visual imaginations, sometimes from a mix of both. Schönberg remembered the cigarette girls emerging from their workplace in Bizet's *Carmen*, and kept that image in mind when he was writing "The End of the Day", the number which opened the original musical by showing workers bursting from Monsieur Madeleine's factory. But whatever their genesis, scenes and songs always had to advance the plot and maintain the musical's momentum. "Story-telling is primary, secondary, and it would be 'furthery', if that word existed." said Boublil.

A word much used by Schönberg is "implacable", by which he means that a work of art, whether a story or an opera, a sculpture or a song, ideally has a sort of inevitability about it, "like an arrow going to its target the only way it can". That was his aim in creating the score for *Les Misérables*, and the consensus of those who have heard or performed it is that he succeeded.

But who, in France, wanted to know? "We did feel we'd done something good and quite innovative," said Boublil, but the two men were, they felt, "shoemakers in a country where everyone went barefoot". In any case, the genre to which *Les Mis* belongs was, and still is, hard to define. People knew what opera and operetta were – but this? Even Boublil found the form, which he and Schönberg seemed to have pioneered, difficult to categorize: "Pop opera sounds wrong for *Les Mis*. Opera is too pretentious, Musical isn't exactly right either."

Les Misérables

The Original French Concept Album.

Tragédie musicale de Alain Boublil et Claude-Michel Schönberg d'apres l'œuvre de Victor-Hugo.
Musique de Claude-Michel Schönberg. Textes Alain Boublil et Jean-Marc Natel.

Première « hugolienne » au Palais des Sports

Triomphe pour Hossein avec les « Misérables » chantés

Les Misérables » *Un triomphe pour Hossein*

THEATRE

« Les Misérables »
(enchaînés et déchaînés)

Le Monde

COMÉDIE MUSICALE

« Les Misérables »
mis en scène par Robert Hossein

Still, a demo tape of the finished piece was made, with Schönberg himself at the piano singing both male and female parts. Yet there was no progress at all until the collaborators made contact via Europe One Radio with the celebrated director Robert Hossein, who agreed to listen to a cassette of the show. He announced that he was doing so only out of curiosity and had no intention of staging it. "But," recalled Schönberg, "he sat down and was very quiet, and for two hours he didn't say anything. Then he stood up and said, 'OK guys, I'm going to do your show.' He loved it."

Loved it enough to stage the musical in September 1980, again as a series of linked tableaux, in a Palais des Sports which had an unexpected gap in its season between *Holiday on Ice* and the arrival of the Moscow State Circus. That left three months for Hossein's staging of *Les Mis*, and, as it turned out, three months were not enough and the show sold out.

It had had its problems. Not long before the first preview, a panicky call reached Andrew Bruce, one of Britain's leading sound designers. He had worked with Boublil and Schönberg on an album of the show recorded with a French cast in studios in Wembley, and now he was needed to sort out radio microphones that were bewildering the French technicians. He and a colleague arrived in Paris a day later to find chaos ("the score was played at a deafening volume, the libretto and lyrics were inaudible, little was going on except performers yelling at each other"), which resulted in Hossein departing in a huff.

But three days later, Hossein returned to find all problems had been solved and to give a public dressing-down to the head of Europe One Radio ("he was apoplectic, striding up and down, raging, frothing at the mouth") for having wasted so much time. Nor was he pleased when, thanks to the testing of a transmitter on the Eiffel Tower, interference made those radio microphones unusable at the first preview. He went onstage and gruffly ordered the audience to go home, which they mostly did not, staying until the interference stopped an hour and a half later and actually leaving at one o'clock in the morning.

They clearly loved the production, as did Bruce himself. It began spectacularly, with prisoners thrusting their hands through a gigantic grille that then rose to reveal a stage that remained bare afterwards. The sound designer, who was to add the first English-speaking productions of *Les Mis* to credits that already included *Cats* and *Evita*, found it hugely impressive: "It was so epic. And there was this fantastic music. It was the most spine-tingling thing I'd seen since *A Chorus Line* at Drury Lane."

In those three months some 500,000 people packed into the arena, and even before its opening the cast album had sold over 250,000 copies, thanks to Boublil's words, Schönberg's music, and orchestrations by the British composer, arranger and conductor, John Cameron, that have since been heard all over the world. "It was a huge success," recalled Schönberg, "but when it was finished, it was finished."

Or was it? Much later, the collaborators heard from the French Society of Writers that a British producer called Cameron Mackintosh, of whom they knew little, except that he had staged a musical unpromisingly titled *Cats*, was looking for them. And on 4 February 1983 they met him for lunch in Paris. "We didn't know it," said Schönberg, "but it was the most important day of our lives."

Opposite: A page from the brochure of the original Paris production of the musical, which was two years in the making.

Above, left: *Les Misérables* was originally released as a French-language concept album in 1980 with a cover based on the illustration of Cosette by Émile Bayard.

Above, right: Headline cuttings from 1980 French newspapers, in which Robert Hossein's direction received rave reviews.

CHAPTER 2

Hugo & His France

When the French author André Gide was asked to name his nation's supreme poet, his now-famous answer was: "Victor Hugo – hélas!" And, yes, his *Les Misérables* is not only on every reading list, but it is also, in every sense of those adjectives, the mightiest, weightiest work of a writer who came to see himself, and was seen by his countrymen, as much more than a novelist or poet. He was a statesman and a prophet, uttering on the past, present and future of his country with the authority of an Isaiah, Daniel or St Paul.

His own life stretched from 1802 to 1885. This meant that he and his Jean Valjean lived through an historical period when, as André Maurois was to write in his *History of France*, the nation was "still trembling from the impact of the Revolution on the Old Regime" and "in a turmoil of passions".

By the "Revolution" Maurois meant the bloody and turbulent events that occurred between 1789 and 1795 and which saw the declaration of France's first republic and the guillotining of thousands. Theatregoers often assume that the uprising in the musical of *Les Mis* involves this period, but that is not so. Yet what brought students and workers to the Paris barricades in 1832 – the year and the event that Hugo and, consequently, Boublil and Schönberg made the climax of their respective works – was the long-term result of the French Revolution. By then much had happened, but much still remained unresolved.

Napoleon had come and gone, as had Louis XVIII, the brother of the executed Louis XVI. Charles X had followed, ruling a fractious and divided nation until 1830, when his high-handed and oppressive measures provoked the July revolution. Charles was forced to abdicate, and Louis-Philippe was invited to take the throne. But tensions and inequalities between the classes remained. Economic depression came to both town and country. By 1832 the Paris poor were devastated by an outbreak of cholera and the disease carried off General Lamarque, who was seen as the enemy of the royalists and the friend of the people. His funeral triggered the June uprising and the erection of the barricades that are described in Hugo's novel and recreated in Boublil and Schönberg's musical. Some 800 people were killed or wounded in those June days and unrest continued until beyond 1848, the year when there was revolution and fear of revolution throughout Europe.

Where was Hugo himself on 5 June 1832? In Paris's Tuileries, writing a play, when he heard the sound of gunfire coming from the Les Halles district. He hurried there, to find barricades erected and himself trapped in an alley called the Passage du Saumon. Rioters were at one end, government troops at

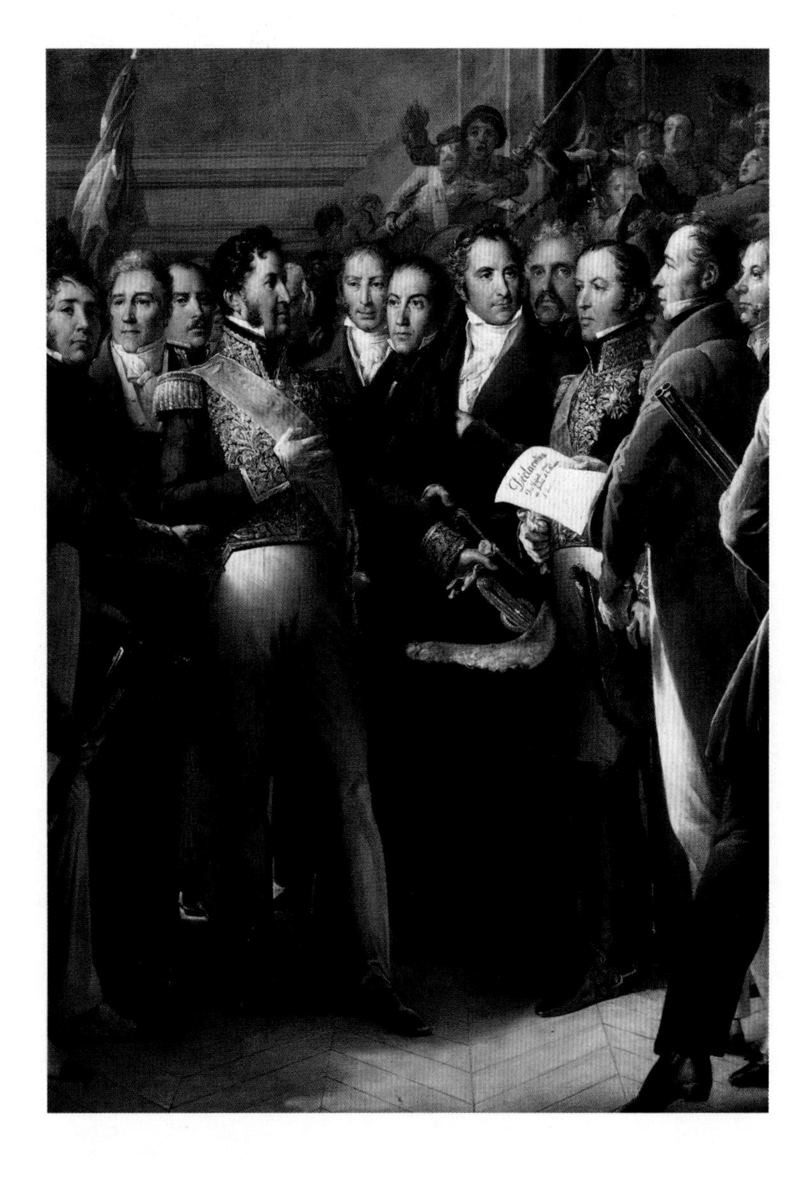

Left, below: When Charles X abdicated following the French Revolution in July 1830, he expressed a wish that his 10-year-old grandson, Henri, should be his successor. However, the Chamber of Deputies decided in favour of Louis Philippe, who for 11 days had acted as regent and whose liberal policies had earned him popularity with the masses. In this detail from François Gérard's 1836 painting, members of the Chamber of Deputies are seen approaching Louis Philippe with the declaration that he is to be the new French king.

Right: An engraving showing a guided tour of the sewers in Rue Laffitte, Paris in 1865. Following a cholera outbreak in the city in 1832, which claimed the lives of many of its poor inhabitants, the sewage system was modernized. Sewers feature in *Les Misérables*, when the character Valjean uses them as an escape route.

Below: *My Destiny*, 1857 (pen, ink, wash and gouache) by Victor Hugo. This work was the inspiration for the vortex in the Soliloquy scene in the 25th anniversary production of *Les Misérables*.

the other. Firing began and bullets were exchanged for a quarter of an hour while Hugo flattened himself against a wall between two shop-fronts. Back home with his diary, he called the uprising "a folly drowned in blood", adding that a republic should come organically, "of its own free will".

Who was Victor Hugo? He was the son of a general and had been a precocious boy, composing a tragedy in verse at the age of 14, founding a periodical called *Le Conservateur Litteraire* when he was 17, and writing poems galore. His first poetic collection was published in 1820, when he was just 20, earning him a royal pension. Fame soon followed, never deserting the author who would write *The Hunchback of Notre Dame*, the 1830 play *Hernani* and, late in his life, *Les Misérables*.

Initially, his sympathies were royalist and his politics the conservative ones of his class, but he was also much affected by the questioning, liberating spirit of nineteenth-century romanticism and was increasingly seen as a liberal and a rebel. Yet he remained avid for recognition by the French establishment and, in 1841, became one of the 40 "immortals" in France's pre-eminent cultural institution, the Académie Française.

Hugo was always contradictory, hard to categorize, something of a maverick. He was arrogant and often tyrannical in his personal dealings, yet his Christian beliefs were strong and his empathy with the underdog

Left: A photograph of Victor Hugo (1802-85), taken in 1864 by Ghémar Frères.

Below: Illustrations by Valnay of the play of *Les Misérables*, adapted for the stage by Victor Hugo's son, Charles, at the Théâtre de la Porte Saint-Martin, Paris, March 1878.

Opposite, right: A street scene showing the barricade erected in Paris's rue Saint-Maur-Popincourt during the uprising in 1848.

Opposite, left: More than two million people gathered to watch Victor Hugo's funeral procession from the Arc de Triomphe down the Champs-Elysées to the Panthéon on 31 May 1885.

equally so. As he grew older, he moved towards the Left, declaring himself a republican, and, when Louis-Napoleon seized power in 1851, he denounced him as a traitor, tried to provoke uprisings, visited barricades, and when he learned that orders had been given to shoot him, he fled Paris for Belgium and then, despite his Anglophobia, for British territory: the Channel Islands.

First in Jersey, and then in Guernsey, where he stayed from 1855 to 1870, he became the inspirational voice of France in exile, the literary counterpart of Charles de Gaulle during the Second World War. And he was still living in Guernsey when his masterpiece, *Les Misérables*, was published.

He had begun the novel in 1845, giving it a working title of *Jean Tréjean*, soon to be changed to *Les Misères*, the wretched, and eventually to *Les Misérables*, whose meaning is both "the poor" and "the bad". He had worked on it sporadically, but then, in 1861, he took the almost completed manuscript to Belgium, went to the fields where Waterloo had been fought, and, he claimed, finished it there. A deal with a Belgian publisher for an astonishing 300,000 francs followed. No fewer than nine translators went to work, and in 1862 the book was published in successive sections in cities ranging from London to Rio, St Petersburg to Naples. In Paris it was a sensation even before it appeared. Factory workers had reportedly set up subscriptions to acquire what would otherwise have cost them several weeks' wages.

For Hugo, never a man to undersell himself, it was "the social and historical drama of the nineteenth century", a modern counterpart of Dante's *Inferno*,

French but also international. It was, he told his Italian publisher, "written for everyone". It was for the world, and the world responded, troops in America's civil war reputedly carrying copies of the book in their knapsacks.

Not everyone was impressed – copies were publicly burned in Spain, and the book itself was proscribed by Pope Pius IX. In an odd, suggestive pre-echo of what was to happen when the musical opened in London, there was also resistance from the French opinion-formers, sometimes on aesthetic grounds, sometimes on moral or political ones. Hugo's critic friend, Alphonse de Lamartine, attacked the book for infecting the masses with a murderous idealism, while the poet Baudelaire, described it in print as "edifying", but privately called it an "unspeakably foul and stupid book".

Today it seems an extraordinary achievement. Yes, the narrative is packed with absurd coincidences, but the novel has the sweep, the authority, the majesty to carry the reader through unlikely happenings and irrelevant homilies alike. "Nowadays it can be discarded as old-fashioned, especially in France," said Alain Boublil, "but that's rubbish to me. It has a power and a passionate flow that few could use without becoming ridiculous. It's flowery, it's inflated, it's grandiose, but to me it's wonderful."

It is also so revealing about Hugo himself that it is sometimes described as autobiographical. The writer admitted that Marius was a self-portrait. After all, he himself had been a bold young idealist who had fallen desperately in love with one Adèle Foucher and, despite her parents' resistance, married her. One also senses a personal grief in his description of the death of Fantine. Leopoldine, his favourite daughter and someone he "loved beyond the power of words to express", drowned in a sailing accident in 1843.

Obviously, there is also much of himself in Valjean. Like his Valjean, the writer saved a wronged girl from a certain prison sentence by telling the police that they should have arrested the gentleman, not her.

Hugo returned to Paris in 1870. Huge crowds greeted him at the Gare du Nord. He became a deputy in the National Assembly, made an ill-received speech advocating partnership with Germany in a United States of Europe, resigned, and had little political impact afterwards. Nevertheless, he was still a legend, and at his death, the pauper's coffin in which he had asked to be buried brought over two million people to watch its slow passage from the Arc de Triomphe down the Champs-Elysées to the Panthéon.

CHAPTER 3

Enter Cameron Mackintosh

In the autumn of 1982 a young director called Peter Farago, who had worked with success at various British theatres, brought Cameron Mackintosh the original French concept album of *Les Mis,* hoping that Mackintosh would give it a British stage premiere. The producer agreed to listen to it but said that choosing a director was another issue. Knowing Paris's reputation as a graveyard for anything theatrical other than opera, operetta or straight drama, he privately thought, "A French musical? That sounds like a contradiction in terms."

But a few days later he was at home and doing nothing in particular, so he played the cassette, starting (he was to recall) at 11.03 in the morning, and by 11.20, when he had reached the fourth track, he was hooked.

Though he had not read Hugo's novel, he had seen the most famous of the many movies adapted from it, the one in which Charles Laughton's Javert famously upstages Fredric March's Valjean. "I went, wow! The smell of the film came back to me as I listened. It was the most exciting theatre music I'd heard since the original album of *Evita*. In fact, I was so excited I didn't want to get to the end of it on my own."

Already eager to produce the musical, that evening he took the album along to Alan Jay Lerner, a great friend since Mackintosh had produced Lerner's own restaging of *My Fair Lady* and introduced the great writer and lyricist to his eighth and last wife, Liz Robertson, who had played Eliza in that revival. Though both of them were thrilled by the score, Lerner told Mackintosh that he would not be the right person to adapt Boublil's words. "I write about dreamers, not ordinary people," he told the producer, referring to *Camelot*, *Gigi*, and *Brigadoon*, as well as *My Fair Lady*.

A choice of lyricist would have to wait, but Mackintosh instantly knew whom he wanted to stage the show. It would not be Farago, but Trevor Nunn, who had just directed the hugely successful *Cats* for him, which proved that Nunn, then artistic director of the Royal Shakespeare Company (RSC), could handle an ambitious musical. Equally, the earlier production of Charles Dickens' *Nicholas Nickleby* that he and John Caird had triumphantly staged for the RSC in 1980 showed he could stage an epic story adapted from a major nineteenth-century novel. There was nobody better equipped to tackle *Les Misérables*.

But first Mackintosh had to track down the authors, Alain Boublil and Claude-Michel Schönberg. After making a number of enquiries, they met for lunch in Paris on 4 February. As Mackintosh remembers the occasion,

Opposite: Cameron Mackintosh in New York for the original Broadway production of *Les Misérables* in 1987.

Above, left: Claude-Michel Schönberg and Alain Boublil during rehearsals, New York, 1987.

Above, right: Pages from the prompt script used by the stage manager, London, 1985.

Below: Trevor Nunn, James Fenton, John Caird and Cameron Mackintosh at a working lunch, Newbury, England, July 1984.

an urbane lyricist did most of the talking while the composer pretended he did not speak English until the end of the meal, "when I realized he had understood everything and was as sharp as a razor". As he also remembers it, the two Frenchmen were surprised to find that Mackintosh did not simply want to buy their work from them and hand it over to a British team. In maybe the most important decision the producer has ever made, he told Boublil and Schönberg he would only produce the show if they brought their distinctive creative skills to its English adaptation and were part of its development from start to finish – and, making a decision that was equally important for them, they agreed.

Schönberg would continue to provide music that, thanks also to John Cameron's powerful, punchy yet sensitive orchestrations, managed to serve the story yet appeal to contemporary tastes. But who would adapt Boublil's carefully chosen words and wonderfully well-shaped libretto? Sheldon Harnick, best known for his lyrics for *Fiddler on the Roof*, was unimpressed. He wrote Mackintosh what the producer remembers as a rather rude letter, dismissing the score as French euroschlock. But when the producer sought advice from Howard Ashman, whose *Little Shop of Horrors* he had produced off-Broadway, that lyricist cheered him by calling *Les Mis* "a marvellous show, one of the most original he'd ever heard". However, the job was offered to an Englishman: James Fenton, the poet and drama critic, who had just written what Mackintosh thought was a brilliant libretto for Jonathan Miller's daring reinvention of Verdi's *Rigoletto* set in New York's Little Italy in the 1950s.

Fenton agreed to join the *Les Mis* team on the somewhat unusual condition that he could start work on the project by reading and pondering the novel on a working holiday spent paddling a canoe through the Borneo jungle. And after a long period of pondering and balancing his priorities, so did Nunn. However, Nunn made his consent provisional on two conditions. First, *Les Mis* must initially be presented at the RSC's London home, the Barbican. Second, John Caird, with whom he had staged a memorable revival of *Peter Pan* as well as *Nicholas Nickleby*, must be his co-director. Mackintosh happily agreed. Caird had just successfully staged his production of Andrew Lloyd Webber's *Song & Dance*. And producing with the RSC meant that, though everyone hoped that *Les Mis* would transfer to the West End, it would not open cold there, but would have the imprimatur, input and stylistic strengths of one of the most admired companies in the western world.

Mackintosh had his conditions, too. Determined to bring all the disciplines of a full-scale commercial musical to the show, he insisted on the participation of a top musical theatre creative team and cast, a number of whom Nunn had worked with at the RSC or when he staged *Cats*. Sound designer Andrew Bruce joined the team, as did Britain's premier lighting designer David Hersey, costume designer, Andreane Neofitou and John Napier, who had won Tony® Awards for his designs for *Nicholas Nickleby* and *Cats* and was asked to create designs for *Les Mis* that would fit the stage of the Palace Theatre, where *Les Mis* had an option to move after the Barbican.

Les Mis was clearly a risky enterprise, but then so was *Cats*. As would be Mackintosh's next collaboration with Boublil and Schönberg, *Miss Saigon*: "How could anyone expect a musical based on T. S. Eliot's cat poems or the Vietnam war to be popular?" Forty-odd years as a London producer has taught him that projects that seem safe may turn out to be the opposite.

The eldest of the three sons of a Maltese mother and an Anglo-Scottish

Above, left: The original Little Cosette Zoe Hart, seen here in the classic pose echoing the original Émile Bayard illustration for the novel.

Above, right: Opening night programme for *Les Misérables* at the Barbican, October 1985.

Opposite: A Barbican production meeting, 1985, with (clockwise from the left) Herbert Kretzmer, John Caird, Trevor Williamson, Simon Opie, Trevor Nunn, Martin Koch, John Napier, Howard Harrison, Cameron Mackintosh, David Hersey and Andrew Bruce.

father, Cameron had initially thought the musical theatre "soppy and sissy", only to change his mind one afternoon in 1954. It was then that the eight-year-old boy was taken to a performance of Julian Slade's *Salad Days*, a musical that involved a pair of improbably innocent lovers needing a job that would keep their parents off their backs, and a magic piano that set everyone dancing. He stayed behind after the show and introduced himself to Slade, who was in the orchestra pit and showed him how that mysterious piano worked. From that moment on Mackintosh was obsessed with the theatre and determined to make a career in it: so much so that his nickname at school was Darryl F. Mackintosh, after the Hollywood mogul, Darryl F. Zanuck.

Cameron Mackintosh left school at the age of 17, enrolling in a stage management course at the Central School of Speech and Drama that he found so unfulfilling he dropped out, and managed to get a job on *Camelot* at the Theatre Royal, Drury Lane. There, he worked backstage with props, cleaned carpets and washed glasses in the dress circle bar where one day audiences would gather in the interval of his own production of *Miss Saigon* and *My Fair Lady*. Soon, he was an assistant stage manager (and actor) on the tour of Lionel Bart's *Oliver!*, a deputy stage manager on *110 in the Shade*, a now-forgotten American musical that came to the West End in 1967, and, aged just 20, among the men reopening a tiny theatre in Henley-on-Thames. And there he and his then producing partner, Robin Alexandar, launched themselves into theatre management with a production of William Douglas Home's comedy, *The Reluctant Debutante* in 1967 – which he certainly was not!

Then came the setbacks and struggles that seem *de rigueur* for any theatrical figure. *Anything Goes*, which Mackintosh brought to the Saville in 1969, lost him, the bank and his backers, some £45,000, a considerable sum in an era when a West End play could be staged for £5000. A touring production of *Mrs Dale's Diary*, a play derived from a popular radio soap, was also a failure, convincing him that straight plays were not his forte. But Julian Slade, who had never forgotten his encounter with the boy Cameron, came to the rescue. Mackintosh toured a revival of his smash hit *Salad Days*, and then came numerous tours of Stephen Schwartz's *Godspell*. In 1972, Mackintosh and Slade's friend, Veronica Flint-Shipman, presented the London premiere of *Trelawny*, based on Pinero's play about nineteenth-century theatre, *Trelawny of the Wells*. Though it was only a modest success, this Julian Slade musical established Mackintosh as a potential player at the age of 25.

Gradually, he became a major one. The following year he produced his first original musical, *The Card*, based on Arnold Bennett's novel about an opportunist boy's rise to provincial power that brought Jim Dale to the West End and, importantly, three years later, he brought the snappy revue, *Side by Side by Sondheim*, to London. Not only did it receive rave reviews and make money, but it also launched a lasting friendship with the American composer and librettist whose work the show was celebrating

and whose *Follies* Mackintosh would bring to the West End in 1987. For Stephen Sondheim, Mackintosh was and is "an overexcited, breathlessly and unabashedly enthusiastic child in the playground of musical theatre – if you took all his money away, he would simply start again".

That catches the character of a man who has continued to exude energy, ebullient optimism and an almost boyish delight in the theatre into his seventies. He has had his less fortunate projects, but his London and Broadway productions of *Cats*, *Les Mis*, *Miss Saigon*, *The Phantom of the Opera* and *Mary Poppins* have much more than compensated for any lack of success. Indeed, *Cats* was London's longest-running musical until *Les Mis* overtook it, and was Broadway's record-holder until *Phantom* arrived and on 9 January 2006 became the longest-running show in Broadway history, which together with *Les Mis* gave Mackintosh the top three of all time. Add West End transfers of the National Theatre productions of *Carousel* and *Oklahoma!* that had been staged with the help of the Mackintosh Foundation, and his two new stagings of *My Fair Lady*, and it is not surprising that the *New York Times* has called Mackintosh "the most successful, influential and powerful producer in the world".

What's the secret, apart from a willingness to look beyond the predictable and familiar? Sir Cameron, as Mackintosh became in 1996, has said that he seeks projects that exhilarate him, shows that stir the emotions, musicals that send an audience home feeling moved and even changed. "It doesn't matter if the material is dark or light," he said. "What has to grab me when I read it is the story, lyrics that tell a story, and the characters in the story. If I don't relate to the characters myself, it doesn't mean the show won't work, it means I'm not the right person to be producing it. And the music has to tell the story, too, and be wonderfully dramatic as well as theatrical."

Mackintosh is especially drawn to stories in which seemingly ordinary people do extraordinary things, as they do in *Les Mis* itself. But he never dreamed that the show would prove to be the success it has or even match Lloyd Webber's relatively dark *Evita*. Indeed, he thought it would be "wonderful" if *Les Mis* lasted two years, a length of run considered pretty good before the 1980s.

With that relatively modest expectation, he rasied the money to match the £300,000 that the RSC agreed to contribute "in kind" for the first production of *Les Mis*, plus another £300,000 if the transfer from the Barbican Centre to the Palace Theatre in London's West End occurred as planned. Though some ideologues criticized a partnership between a subsidized company and a commercial producer, it proved a very good deal for the RSC, which has received £19 million since the show's inception and, in 2012, was still getting some £400,000 a year. Among *Les Mis*'s achievements, therefore, is helping to keep an internationally important company off the financial rocks that have sometimes threatened to sink it.

Below: Cameron Mackintosh with Trevor Nunn and John Caird outside the Theatre Royal, Sydney, 1987.

Opposite: The London cast in a Paris street scene, 2007.

CHAPTER 4

The Original Dream Team

The making of large-scale musicals is usually a long, difficult business, but in the case of *Les Mis* it was especially so. The original French text clearly needed major restructuring for a musical-theatre audience in London and, if all went well, for New York. For English-speaking audiences, the story had to be sharpened, links between events clarified, and the characters strengthened.

As Caird says, that story is far simpler than that of his and Nunn's great success, *Nicholas Nickleby*. For all his digressions, Hugo's prime focus was Valjean's journey to a redemption that is spiritual as well as moral. Caird, Nunn and Fenton were initially most interested in Hugo's political views and wondered if it would be possible to diminish the significance of God, a Being that, as Caird wryly remarks, was not wholly congenial to the RSC in its then Leftist days.

But the three men agreed with Boublil and Schönberg that this would be unfaithful to an author whose overall voice and, sometimes, actual words they wanted the musical to project. So when the dying Valjean and the ghost of Fantine declare that "to love another person is to see the face of God", as well as when students sing about the need for social change, they are representing an invisible Hugo.

As Nunn said, the question the novel and the musical ask is both religious and political: "Do we so believe in an omniscient God that we must leave the social conditions we live in to that God or, realizing we're surrounded by justice and inequality, take arms and change them?"

Fenton got down to business, working with Boublil and Caird and communicating regularly with Nunn. An early decision was to create a 15-minute prologue, complete with motifs from the Schönberg numbers that would appear later in the musical, showing what happened to Valjean between his release from the chain gang to his becoming the mayor of Montreuil-sur-Mer. Another major decision came as a result of, as Nunn puts it, "two extraordinary pieces of melodic material, both for Fantine, being finished in the first quarter of the show".

The now-famous number that had the doomed girl dreaming of another, better life would remain where it was, but Boublil and Schönberg's "Misère", originally Fantine's song about poverty, would become "On My Own", a second-act lament sung by a different character: Thénardier's daughter Eponine, who has moved to the Paris slums and fallen hopelessly in love with Marius. And Marius himself acquired a song that everyone agreed that the character needed, one expressing the guilt of surviving his

Left: Trevor Nunn directing rehearsals at the Barbican, 1985, with Michael Ball in the background.

Above: Frances Ruffelle as Eponine, singing "On My Own", is dwarfed by the scale of John Napier's set, London, 1985.

fallen comrades, "Empty Chairs at Empty Tables".

So the work continued, but slowly, far too slowly. As the time for rehearsals approached, the show had been effectively restructured but the lyrics were still a first draft and, in Mackintosh and Nunn's view, not right for a popular musical. As Nunn said, "James Fenton is a poet, a brilliant poet, but his involvement with *Les Misérables* is proof positive that poetry and lyrics don't necessarily connect. To get the word on the stress in the music, to get the vowel that is absolutely 'singable' as if it was natural, require a completely different habit of mind."

"It was a crisis," recalled Mackintosh. "Casting was under way, I had pressed the button for a huge musical but we didn't have one single word an actor could really act. Actors were being auditioned with material that was not going to be in the show. The show had been announced for the autumn and we didn't have a usable libretto. Yes, it was scary."

Inevitably, he and Nunn decided they had to replace a poet who had, as everyone concedes, done much to establish the show's architecture and some of whose words are still to be heard in it. Fenton gave way to Herbert Kretzmer, a critic and lyricist who had created English versions of songs, notably "Yesterday When I Was Young", for Charles Aznavour.

Months before, he had been to see Mackintosh hoping the impresario might consider mounting a new version of a 1960s musical based on J. M. Barrie's *Admirable Crichton*, whose lyrics he had written. Though Mackintosh remembered liking them a lot, the answer to that was "No", and Kretzmer was walking out of Mackintosh's office when he told the producer of his work for the French singer: "In those 30 seconds my life changed. Cameron reeled round the office and fell backwards against his own door and said, 'Good God, you didn't?' His enthusiasm couldn't have been more exuberantly expressed."

That encounter had lodged in Mackintosh's mind, with the result that in the spring of 1985 Kretzmer found himself engaged on a task that was far more demanding than he expected. Some of Boublil's lyrics, such as "I Dreamed a Dream", are directly translatable into English whereas a song like the untranslatable "La Nuit" had to become "Lovely Ladies" to convey the dramatic mood. Fenton's poetic English words had to be reinvented in a

Above, left: Herbert Kretzmer, who replaced James Fenton as lyricist in spring 1985. He has received numerous awards for his work, including an OBE and the Chevalier de l'Ordre des Arts et des Lettres.

Above: Alun Armstrong and Sue Jane Tanner as Thénardier and his wife, in rehearsal in 1985. Along with Roger Allam, these were the only cast members to be chosen from the RSC.

way that would express character, push on the story, resonate with an English audience and fit Schönberg's music. Recalling the challenges, Kretzmer ruefully quotes his fellow-lyricist Don Black, who once said that writing lyrics was "as painful as doing your own root-canal work".

As it got closer to August 1985, when rehearsals belatedly started, Kretzmer was toiling in his Knightsbridge flat for up to 20 hours a day and often in the company of John Caird, with the two men interspersing their work on the lyrics with meals of smoked salmon bought daily from Harrods. They were still revising or creating new lyrics even when rehearsals were under way and it had become increasingly clear that the characters of Javert and Valjean needed more building up. "Stars", in which the policeman compares his own rigid beliefs to the order he sees in the heavens, was a late addition. So was "Bring Him Home", a song it had been decided that Valjean, who had far too little to do during the long barricade scene, needed before he rescued the wounded Marius.

Initially, that number foxed Kretzmer. The lyricist was in despair when, after a late-night session just 17 days before the show's first preview, Caird left the flat remarking "sounds like a prayer to me". There, in five words, was the solution. That very night, between 1.00 am and breakfast, Kretzmer wrote what is perhaps the most beautiful of lyrics. However, the important "On My Own" proved so intransigent that Kretzmer, who had toiled on it for five months, asked for assistance from Nunn and Caird. And on the musical's CDs and DVDs they share the credit with Kretzmer for words that Nunn recalled scribbling on a scrap of paper late in the evening while he and Caird discussed the show in their favoured restaurant, Joe Allen's, in central London. Frances Ruffelle, who was playing Eponine and had been anxiously asking "Got my lyric?", finally received it.

Meanwhile, casting was at last complete. Initial auditions, which began with members of the RSC, had been a mixed success, since few of the company's actors sang well enough to get a role. In the end, only three were chosen, though for important characters: Roger Allam for Javert, Alun Armstrong for Thénardier and Sue Jane Tanner for Madame Thénardier. Casting had continued in London and in equally vital cases had proved difficult. Not until Nunn gave the lyricist Tim Rice a description of Valjean – a convict, strong, tough, yet a beautiful singer – did he hear of the Irish tenor, Colm Wilkinson. Wilkinson duly gave a rendering of "Anthem", a song from Rice and Abba's *Chess*, which Caird remembered as "just blowing us away". He was promptly cast in the role, but a performer capable of playing Fantine proved even more elusive. Rehearsals had already started when the American actress Patti LuPone assumed the one role that the team had failed to cast in Britain.

Rehearsals began and continued in true RSC fashion. Nunn had directed Shakespeare and other classic authors for the RSC with such success that at the age of 28 he succeeded Peter Hall as the company's artistic director. However, he has always felt that the barrier between serious drama and good musicals – "the word 'legitimate' says it all, implying musical theatre is illegitimate" – should be knocked down as artificial and snobbish.

Caird, the son of an Oxford theologian, who was Nunn's associate director at the RSC in the 1980s, had also proved himself skilful at staging ambitious work, He directed some 20 productions for the company, including a *Romeo and Juliet* featuring Daniel Day-Lewis and Roger Allam. He is also an able pianist, musically adept enough to have staged *Song & Dance* in the West End for Cameron Mackintosh and Andrew Lloyd Webber. And when he first heard Schönberg's music, listening to a cassette of *Les Mis* as he drove home after staging a *Romeo and Juliet* in Newcastle, he was "completely spellbound within minutes".

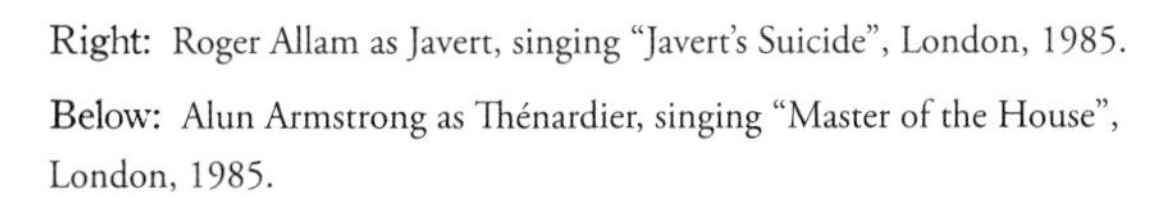

Right: Roger Allam as Javert, singing "Javert's Suicide", London, 1985.

Below: Alun Armstrong as Thénardier, singing "Master of the House", London, 1985.

The two men are close friends and, like Boublil and Schönberg, unafraid to challenge each other's ideas yet so effective together they struck Kretzmer as "symbiotic figures, the same man – they'd finish each other's sentences". And they were determined to bring the same RSC disciplines, the same seriousness, to *Les Mis* as they had to Shakespeare. That meant asking their performers to immerse themselves in French history and ideas and ensuring that the performers fully inhabited their characters. Thoughts and feelings had to be so thoroughly thought and felt that they seamlessly became words and, this time, sung words. As Caird said, there is nothing worse in a musical than an actor seeming suddenly to say, "Oh, I feel a number coming on". As Nunn added, "the language is heightened, but if you simply recite or sing it, it will become dull and tedious – performers must get to the point where they feel that they themselves are creating the lyrics and the melody."

Nunn and Caird started a longer-than-usual rehearsal period with a talk about Hugo, his France and his novel that Nick Allott, then Mackintosh's executive producer and now his managing director, remembered lasting from 10.30 to 3.30 and ending with the company in stitches after one of the boys alternating the role of Gavroche cheekily asked, "Would you mind saying that again?" Then came exercises and improvisations; some designed to bond actors, some to help them deepen their characters, some simply to relieve stress.

It seemed important to Nunn and Caird to explain why the students were angry enough to rebel. The impoverished and the destitute had to be brought onstage and to life. Ensemble performers playing beggars or whores were asked to give them names and create background stories for them. The company was split into groups and asked to improvise and perform sequences drawn from the novel: "We wanted to make them feel much more like real nineteenth-century people," recalled Caird. "To be poorer, needier and more desperate than well-fed twentieth-century actors could easily imagine."

Michael Ball, playing Marius, remembered lighter exercises, including one in which the cast was asked to perform cartoon actors and he became Popeye. By that time, he said, performers were wondering if such exercises were continuing because new material kept appearing: "There was this wonderful atmosphere of hard work, but we all said, we're doing improvisations so much because the show isn't written." Yet six weeks into rehearsals, things were sufficiently ready for the cast, which numbered 27 yet was required to play well over 100 roles, to move into the now demolished Astoria Theatre. There, a revolving stage had been set up and they could begin to learn what it would be like to act and sing on John Napier's remarkable set.

Right: Rebecca Caine (Cosette), Colm Wilkinson (Valjean) and the company in rehearsal singing "One Day More", London, 1985.

CHAPTER 5

The London Opening

Soon everyone was in the Barbican, holding technical rehearsals and then performing a show on a set that was fundamental to *Les Mis*'s original success. Its revolving stage allowed swift, almost filmic movement between scenes, especially at the beginning, when it turned and turned as the released Valjean seemed to walk or run from place to unwelcoming place. Then there was the simple furniture and the rough-theatre feel that Napier had brought to *Nicholas Nickleby*. Some of the most striking and spectacular effects emerged from a trip that the designer made with Caird and Nunn to Paris streets where barricades actually had or could have been erected.

Left: A number of the props from Act I.

Below: The set designer John Napier during the preparations for the London production.

I remember seeing an authentic bunch of prostitutes in the Rue St-Denis, and I thought it's still going on," recalled Caird. "We went all round the Left Bank, with John Napier taking photographs of cobblestones and huge beams, enormous stanchions, holding up the remaining bits of buildings that were falling down. The Paris set and the barricades were based on those observations."

Born in 1944, Napier originally trained as a sculptor and retains that mindset when he creates the designs that have made his name. As he has said, "I don't think two-dimensionally, as a painter does. I'm trying to bring the stage out to the audience. I think three-dimensionally." He has a strong sense of theatre, which means his sets tend to leave much to the audience's imagination and have non-naturalistic, even surreal aspects. *Cats*, with its wonderfully inventive bric-a-brac for felines to disport on, is the obvious case; but Napier has won major awards for designs ranging from *Peter Pan* to Andrew Lloyd Webber's *Starlight Express*, *King Lear* to *Miss Saigon*.

Certainly, Napier brought his "stylized realism", theatricality and sense of atmosphere to *Les Mis*. The Paris slums were unforgettably evoked by two vast sculptures of ladders, old chairs, wheels, barrels and general junk that trundled out of wings to be linked by a bridge or, for the barricade, to meet, slant and lock together like two sci-fi monsters in a weird, jagged embrace. Equally, David Hersey's lighting proved dramatically effective, whether sunlit day or moonlight, glare or glimmer, was required. And when the action moved to the Paris sewers, Hersey rose wonderfully to the occasion. There, he and Napier evoked a murky, foggy hell and, by isolating the characters with successive circles of light, suggested they were precariously trudging through it.

The two men also brought to life the seemingly "un-stageable" episode in which Javert, freed by the "evil" man he has unceasingly pursued and unable to take this challenge to his implacable beliefs, commits suicide. As the critic J. C. Trewin wrote, "The bridge at the back of the stage rises suddenly.

Above: A newspaper clipping advertising bookings for *Les Misérables*' opening run at the Barbican.

Below: An invitation to the party held on the opening night of the London production of *Les Misérables*, 8 October 1985.

Above: The poster for the original London production of *Les Misérables* at the Barbican Theatre, October 1985.

Below: A ticket stub from the opening night performance at the Barbican.

Background: A scale drawing of John Napier's original set design for the London production of *Les Misérables* that included a central revolve to enable smooth, quick scene changes.

Left: The barricade scene.

Below: Michael Ball as the student rebel Marius singing "Empty Chairs at Empty Tables", London, 1985.

Thanks to the lighting we look at the Seine and the central swirl of water in which Javert sinks. It is a breathtaking, eye-catching effect which may seem simple yet is so complex."

The first previews ran for nearly four hours, so long that Michael Ball recalled hearing the half-hour call for the evening performance while a matinée was still in progress. Cuts continued, even after the preview period, and performers found themselves losing, or in danger of losing, many of their lines. Ball himself threatened to leave the show when he heard that his great number, "Empty Chairs and Empty Tables", might have to be sacrificed: "It wouldn't have affected the story line but it would have neutered Marius." But Mackintosh and the directors had already come to the same conclusion.

However long the show, the preview audiences were clearly gripped and moved. Colm Wilkinson recalled hearing spectators crying even at a technical rehearsal, when the actors were not in costume, and the first paying spectators doing so, too: "I could see them with their heads down and tears streaming down their faces." "At the first preview they were standing and shouting, with their hands over the heads," recalled LuPone. Nunn remembered people shouting "Yes!" at the rousing chorus which had been added to the original show, ending it with a call to arms and, following Hugo himself, the words "tomorrow comes!".

Diana Princess of Wales came to a special charity performance, loved the show, came again, and became a serious fan, telling Mackintosh that she had worn out her cassette of the show and receiving a new one as a gift the next day. Virtually every night there was a standing ovation, something then rare in the British theatre. Alun Armstrong said, "People were going potty, cheering and whistling and jumping to their feet. As far as we were concerned, we were in a hit show."

But were they? Here we come to what is the most notorious but also the

Above: Gavroche, who in the novel is actually revealed as the unloved middle son of the Thénardiers, turned street urchin, on the barricades. The part in the original London production was shared by actors Ian Tucker (seen here) and Oliver Spencer as well as a young girl, Liza Hayden.

most bewildering moment in the history of *Les Mis*. I, myself, remember a first night when the audience was clearly rapt throughout. I glanced at the stranger sitting on my right and she looked the way the earthlings do in *Close Encounters of the Third Kind*, gaping with wonder at the alien spaceship that has just landed. So, I dare say, did I. Ball recalled the second night, often a downbeat occasion, in which "the audience went mental, absolutely beserk".

That ended a strange, seesawing day that had begun so badly that nobody could believe any longer that they were in a hit show. After a particularly joyous first-night party in the Barbican, one apparently crashed by members of the audience who could not bear to leave the theatre, Cameron Mackintosh walked to Piccadilly Circus to pick up the morning papers that had just arrived – "I read reviews by people I knew and in some cases were friends, the blood drained from my face, and I became quite tearful."

Not all were negative. In a particularly eloquent review, the *Financial Times*'s Michael Coveney hailed "a most enjoyable musical" that "occupied brand new ground somewhere between Verdi and Andrew Lloyd Webber". The *Guardian*'s Michael Billington gave the show a mixed review, but the *Daily Telegraph*'s John Barber lamented the "monster show"that had been created from Hugo's "turgid panorama", which ended up "dragging". *The Times*'s highly regarded Irving Wardle felt the show increasingly gave itself up to "spectacle and push-button emotionalism at the expense of character and content". Worse still, the *Daily Mail*'s influential Jack Tinker wrote that the show's creators had tried to "pour the entire Channel through a china teapot", had turned Hugo's "tidal waves of emotions into ripples of cheap sentiment", and, despite some thrilling music, produced a show with little verbal excitement. His review finished by claiming that "*Les Misérables* has, sadly, been reduced to *The Glums*".

Worse was to come on Sunday. True, *The Sunday Times*'s John Peter much admired a "gripping, brilliantly paced and thrillingly organized musical", notable for its "fresh, astringent lyricism" and "masterful theatricality", but he undermined his praise by wondering why so much skill had been lavished on Hugo's "turgid and wobbly tale". The *Sunday Telegraph*'s Francis King wrote of a "lurid Victorian melodrama", and under a headline reading "Victor Hugo on the Garbage Dump", the *Observer*'s Michael Ratcliffe decided that the show's creators had "emasculated Hugo's Olympian perspective and reduced it to the trivializing and tearful aesthetic of rock opera and the French hit parade of 10 or 15 years ago".

The show's creators were devastated, while noting a certain irony in what became a common insult. An RSC employee half-facetiously suggested that the show should be called *The Glums*, after a dim and gloomy family in a once-popular radio show called *Take It From Here*, while Nunn and Caird were wondering if an unwelcoming title should not be changed to *The Outcasts*, *The Fugitive* or *Poverty*, but Mackintosh refused to alter it.

To this day, the reason some critics were so hugely at odds with *Les Mis*'s audiences is debated. Some blame the same cultural snobbery Nunn hoped to counter; some think reviewers were punishing the RSC and its artistic director for daring to tackle a popular musical, perhaps because of Peter Hall's recent disastrous musical foray, *Jean Seberg*, at the National Theatre. Boublil said that he supposed French critics might have been equally dismayed if the show had opened at the Comédie-Française, but still

Above: Diana, Princess of Wales was a huge fan of *Les Misérables*. She is seen here with John Caird attending a performance at the Barbican in October 1985.

Below: Andreane Neofitou's original costume designs for the wedding of Marius and Cosette.

Above: The unemployed and factory workers singing "At the End of the Day", London, 1992.

wondered if Francophobia played a part. Claude-Michel Schönberg, who had been working on the music from 9.00 a.m. to 2.00 a.m. the following morning, was equally dismayed. Whatever the truth, the atmosphere was depressed in the restaurant where the design and marketing firm Dewynters held their traditional post-opening lunch, one aimed at analyzing reviews and formulating strategy. Could a show that had been so badly panned, and had such a small advance, even at the Barbican, possibly transfer to the Palace Theatre in the West End?

Then a producer Caird remembered as "ashen-faced" left the gathering, wanting to "get the worst of it out of the way". After trying several times to phone the Barbican box-office, Cameron Mackintosh finally made contact, and received astonishing news. It had had the busiest day the box-office manager could remember. Some 5,000 tickets had been sold in three hours. There were still long queues at the box-office itself. More staff were needed. As Alun Armstrong remarked, punning on the number that ended the musical, it was a case of "Do You Hear the People Ring?" One ray of critical sunshine did come through at the lunch – an advance copy of Sheridan Morley's rave "Victor Victorious" review for *Punch*. Of all the English critics he became the show's greatest champion.

That sudden, rapid change of fortunes remains, as Kretzmer put it, "one of the theatre's great mysteries, a magical thing". But could the "word of mouth" effect be trusted to last? As Allott, Managing Director of Cameron Mackintosh, said, it would still have been more sensible not to have

Above: Andreane Neofitou's evocative original design for Eponine.

Above, left: David Greer as Enjolras, together with students and citizens performing "Do You Hear the People Sing?", London, 1990.

Left: A London taxi advertising *Les Misérables*, approaching the Palace Theatre, circa 1986.

Following pages: (Left) The original production of *Les Misérables* opened to some negative press reviews after the opening night on 8 October 1985, but the audiences loved it. (Right) The Palace Theatre, London, where *Les Misérables* played from December 1985 to March 2004 before transferring to the Queen's Theatre where it is still running in 2018.

transferred the show. Andrew Lloyd Webber, who had recently bought the Palace Theatre and was thought initially to have disliked *Les Mis*, was willing and even eager to refund the supposedly unreturnable £50,000 deposit that Mackintosh had given him. Moreover, there was virtually no advance at the Palace box-office, and Mackintosh had barely 24 hours to make one of the most fateful decisions of his life, one that Nunn and Caird, Boublil and Schonberg and Kretzmer, still hail as remarkably bold.

That afternoon Mackintosh spoke to the show's major American backers, Elizabeth Williams and Karen Goodwin, pointing out to them that, if *Les Mis* did not transfer, they could have back half the money that they and their investors had put into it. The answer, as he remembered, was, "We'd have shouted at you if you hadn't decided to take it into the West End. We absolutely want to go the whole way." So he announced the coming transfer to the performers, who were understandably worried about their futures, at a morale-boosting drinks that evening.

Les Mis had opened at the Barbican on 8 October, quickly sold out, and on 23 November closed the run that had, Mackintosh observed, brought many people unfamiliar with the RSC, and perhaps some who never normally went to the theatre at all, into that rather forbidding building. There had been substantial cuts to reduce the show's length to three and a half hours. Eight trucks then took Napier's set and other necessities the two miles to the Palace, where it opened on 4 December, by which time it had been cut by another quarter of an hour.

"Fight for a ticket" went up on the Palace frontage, along with a huge reproduction of the original nineteenth-century lithograph of Cosette that has become the show's instantly recognisable symbol all over the world. Scalpers and touts quickly moved in to take advantage. "Get your tickets for *Lesbian Rebels*," Allott remembers hearing one shout. Defying critics, doom-mongers and even its own title, *Les Misérables* had arrived and was not going to disappear.

26—The LONDON STANDARD, WEDNESDAY, OCTOBER 9, 1985

The Critics

Hugo-a-go-go

by MILTON SHULMAN

IF IT were not for the past, the musical would now be in danger of becoming a defunct art-form.

It is the spirit of the 1920s and 1930s as typified in musicals like Me And My Girl, Guys And Dolls and 42nd Street that has attracted recent audiences to the West End.

Les Misérables at the Barbican takes a giant step even further backwards in providing a musical entertainment which in plot, characters, mood, morality and message would have been relished by Drury Lane audiences in the 1890s.

Since the Royal Shakespeare Company has already proved the money-spinning potential of synopsised Dickens, it is entitled to try its luck with the commercialisation of Victor Hugo.

Perhaps one's expectation of something more adventurous and contemporary comes from the use of the word "musical" to popularise what is in essence a light opera, or should one say a glum opera.

The epic account of Jean Valjean's struggle against injustice is 1200 pages long in the newest Penguin edition of the classic and would no doubt take about a week to read aloud.

By filleting it down to three hours on the stage, including 25 songs, its French adaptors, Alain Boublil and Claude-Michel Schonberg, have stripped the story not only of its many digressions but of its social significance, its convincing humanity and its questing idealism.

In France, where knowledge of the book is the essence of ...one's education, audi- ...all in for them- ...in this

its ramifications would b... advised to study the pl... outlined in the program... they may find them... baffled by events and... acters that appear ar... appear with the irrelev... rabbits out of a c... magician's hat.

Les Misérables reco... travails of Valjean, w... 19 years in prison be... stole a loaf of bread, ... on his release the c... a priest set him on ... of good deeds and r... ary fervour.

Pursuing him is ... inspector, Javert, ... sonal code about t... of the law is as ... as Valjean's unyie... in moral integrity...

Over the yea... under various ... achieves wealth ... which he uses ... Father Bountif... wretch who cros...

Fantine, one o... with an illegi... Cosette, attract... and results i... Cosette and ev... her lover, Mar... shot on the ... Paris.

While John... give a vivid i... barricades a... dominate the... the story, th... to me to ... indicate th... degradation ... Fantine's d... bed as well ... supplied by ...

The m... Michael ... melodic op... verge of ... The l...

give mature dignity to what might otherwise be dismissed as lachrymose opera but also provide the evening with its ...glimmers of fun. ...Colm Wilkinson ...

...13 OCTOBER 1985 OBSE...

The RSC's musical version of 'Les Mis...

Victor Hu... the garbag...

THE RSC's attempt to stage a three-hour musical of Hugo's enormous novel Les Misérables, write the directors Trevor ...

THEATRE

The Mail on Sunday, October 13, 1985

Part Two

Ingenuity defeated by genius

VIRTUOUS: Colm Wilkinson as Valje...

THEATRE

By KENNETH HURREN

THE Royal Shakespeare Company's grimly spectacular musical **Les Misérables** at the Barbican has such sweeping grandeur it is almost a pleasure to be bored by it.

And that — despite some tenderly affecting romantic moments after the first hour or two — is what you may often be.

Watching it is rather like eating an artichoke: you have to go through an awful lot to get a very little.

Convict

able outcasts of 19th-century Paris.

What we get are the unfleshed bones of the story of Jean Valjean, the parole-jumping convict converted to good works but an eternal fugitive. The stage is awash with unanswered questions, and the telescoped tale is slow to gain dramatic impetus.

Herbert Kretzmer's English lyrics ...

expected him to be borne to heaven by angels in a golden chariot.

That scenic effect is denied us. Others are magnificent.

Put that down to the production team who also worked on Nicholas Nickleby ...

class women to ... The rise and ri... Warren (a busyb... were), financed by ... hungry baronet, s... the censor that th... to wait nearly 30 y...

THE SUNDAY TELEGRAPH OCTOBER 13, 1985

THEATRE FRANCIS KING

GLUM-SHOW

ALTHOUGH it runs for almost 3½ hours, Alain Boublil's and Claude-Michel Schönberg's musical of Victor Hugo's **Les Misérables** ("The Glums") at the Barbican stands in the same relation to the original as a singing telegram to an epic. Given the prolixity of the original, this could hardly be otherwise.

The reduction of a literary mountain to a dramatic molehill has had the unfortunate effect that all the things that, to a modern reader, are least satisfactory in the narrative—improbabilities, sentimentalities, the coincidences that constantly bring the ticket-of-leave man Valjean and the police agent Javert into confrontation—now seem far more glaring. What, in its essentials, we have here is a lurid Victorian melodrama, produced with Victorian lavishness.

In the exaggerated chiaroscuro of David Herse's lighting, the good characters tend to get bathed in a golden light. All the characters get enmeshed, he dies, in the golden syrup of Claude-Michel Schönberg's music, which pours on and on of a seemingly bottomless ...

Visually, with the huge cast swept back and forth across the stage on the ebb and flow of the action, with the revolve constantly substituting one scene for another, and with the barricades coming together literally before one's eyes ...

and the designer, John Napier.

Although he has neither the strength of physique nor the force of personality essential for the role, Colm Wilkinson not merely sings (there is no spoken dialogue) the role of Valjean with eloquence but—far more difficult—brings out all the essential goodness of a much-wronged man. The outstanding voice is that of Patti LuPone as Fantine, the factory-worker forced into prostitution to keep her child. Amplification turns some of the other, less professional, voices into nasal wails.

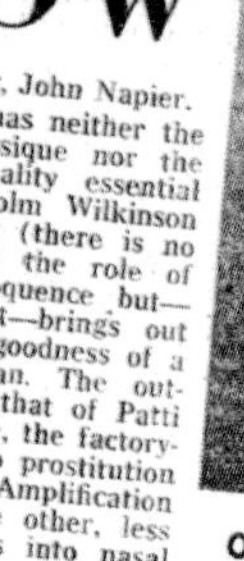

* * *

WILDE titillated his audiences by turning verbal clichés upside down. By turning situational clichés upside down, Shaw achieved the same effect. Thus, whereas fallen women in other plays of the period live out their lives in hapless ignominy, the wages of sin for Mrs Warren of **Mrs Warren's Profession** (Lyttelton) are wealth, power and, above all, happiness.

Again, when Mrs Warren's mathematician daughter, Viv, learns how her mother has earned the money to educate her, she is so far from feeling a more than transient gratitude and pity that she decides that they must stop seeing each other.

There is something chilly and priggish about Viv—mirroring something chilly and priggish about her creator—as she renounces ...

Daily Mail, Wednesday, October 9, 1985

JACK TINKER

At last night's first ...

Les Miserables by Alain Boublil and Claude-Michel Schonberg. Lyrics by Herbert Kretzmer. Music by Claude-Michel Schonberg. The Barbican.

The life and hard times of Les Glums

THE Royal Shakespeare Company have elected to join forces with the commercial theatre and man the barricades to bring the musical version of Victor Hugo's marathon sweep through French social history tothe Barbican. They have, needless to say, more than half an eye on making a killing in the West End later.

There are, however, two major and maybe insurmountable obstacles to this happy outcome and neither of them is the title.

First, there is the sheer scale of the material to be condensed and contained in manageable musical ... paperback translation of ...

into 3½ hours of non-stop operatic treatment, encompassing such grandiose themes as revolution, human degradation, spiritual retribution, obsessive guilt and the triumph of true love might seem like attempting to pour the entire Channel through a China teapot.

In Paris, however, the enterprise has already proved a runaway triumph. The French take their great literature to heart: one small reference to such events in the narrative is enough to sound a clamour of collected national conscience through such an audience. ... with Dickens ...

than Hugo: these shorthand effe... turn this anguished vision of in... twining destinies into a series ... mere coincidences, and his tidal w... of emotions into ripples of ch... sentiment.

The hero Jean Valjean (C... Wilkinson), for example, has ... sooner escaped from the chain ga... than—in no more time than it ta... to sing a song, snatch a ... candlesticks and nip into the w... for a change of costume he is a ... cessful factory owner and mayo... the town.

The second and equally serious ...ficulty this bold Gallic import ...

SHERIDAN MORLEY/THEATRE

Victor Victorious

WE have the musical of the year, if not the half-decade, and it is at the *Barbican*. Not since Sondheim's *Sweeney Todd* back in 1979 has there been a score which soared out from the pit with the blazing theatricality of **Les Misérables**, and to those of my tabloid colleagues already in print with feeble and fainthearted objections to the gloom of Hugo's epic pageant of French life at the beginning of the ...

of which fit like jigsaw pieces into a huge revolutionary pattern. There are songs of love, and war, and death and restoration: there are patter songs, arias, duets and chorus numbers of dazzling inventiveness and variety. For this is not the French *Oliver!* or even the musical ...

time to draw on, it has no book of its own. What it has is a score, and beyond it some thin and sketchy characterisations, but no chance of any plot development that cannot come through song. Again like *Sweeney*, the show exists in the most dangerous area of the stage ...

the Game is one of the ... ly accessible of the nu...

Out at the *Greenwi...* runs, Alan Strachan d... credit than he has els... given for allowing us a ... of Sam Behrman. M... who preferred the initi... essentially the drama... the American theatre ...

THE CAMERON MACKINTOSH ROYAL SHAKESPEARE COMPANY PRODUCTION
THE MUSICAL SENSATION
Les Misérables
"A MUSICAL THAT MAKES HISTORY"
"FIGHT TO GET A TI
PALACE THEATRE
JUBILANT, LAVISH AMBITIOUS AND EXCITING
Les Misérables
LOOK LEFT

CHAPTER 6

Jean Valjean

Les Misérables was already in rehearsal when the assembled cast first heard the lyric that had caused Herbert Kretzmer such trouble and the music that Claude-Michel Schönberg had composed after realizing that the man with the best voice in the company had plenty of words to sing but no aria of his own in the second act.

Bring him home," sang Colm Wilkinson, keeping the words as soft yet intense as the situation demanded. After all, his Jean Valjean was on the barricades, praying for Marius, who was asleep beside him. The boy had to be helped to survive what was sure to be a losing battle. If necessary, he had to be rescued. "Let him live, bring him home, bring him home," ended Wilkinson.

Ken Caswell, playing the Bishop whose gift of candlesticks had changed Valjean's mind, heart and life, broke the awed silence that followed. As Trevor Nunn remembered it, the actor said: "You told us at the beginning that you couldn't keep God out of the show. But you didn't say you'd booked God to sing this song."

The creative team had not erred when, to Wilkinson's consternation, they chose this modest Irishman to play the first of what would be many scores of West End, American and worldwide Valjeans. Not that Wilkinson was wholly unknown. He had played Judas in *Jesus Christ Superstar* onstage and Che in the concept album of *Evita*. He was already celebrated as a solo singer in his native country. But the creative team had previously auditioned the Swedish tenor Tommy Körberg for a role that was proving difficult to cast because of the vocal range it required.

Even though Körberg's voice was not felt to be old enough for the aging Jean Valjean in the second act, it was thanks to him that Schönberg felt ready to alter the baritone role he had written into one suitable for a tenor. Wilkinson impressed everybody with his audition song of "Anthem" from *Chess*. As Michael Coveney later wrote in the *Financial Times*, the Irishman had "a particularly fine and lyrical use of his upper register". Ironically, it was Körberg who had created the role of the Russian grand master in *Chess* and made Wilkinson's audition song a hit.

There, perhaps, is the basic acting requirement for Valjean. He must begin hard, harsh, brutalized by 19 years as a convict, but discover in

Right: Colm Wilkinson (Valjean) and Michael Ball (Marius), London, 1985.

Opposite: Ken Caswell (Bishop of Digne) and Colm Wilkinson (Valjean), London, 1985.

Above, left to right: Danish singer Stig Rossen first appeared as Valjean in London in 1989 and has since sung the role some 1,500 times all over the world; Hans Peter Janssens (Valjean) and Sarah Lane (Cosette), London, 2001; Jung Sung-hwa, played the role of Valjean in both the 2012 and 2015 Korean productions.

himself qualities of goodness, self-sacrifice and love that have been thwarted by imprisonment and ill-treatment. He must embody Hugo's belief that men who have been written off by society can not only be redeemed but also bring light to a dark world. As Wilkinson said, he begins as a savage and ends up "nearly a saint". No wonder, then, that some of the finest stage Valjeans have seen a spirituality in the character and, as they played it, experienced it in themselves.

Almost apologetically, Wilkinson admitted to feeling that there was something fated about his getting a part he never expected. "I come from a Catholic background, but I'm not fanatically Catholic or fanatically religious," he said, "but I did feel very transformed by the part. It just took me over. At times I actually felt I was a channel for that character. It was an out-of-body experience. Not every night, but when it was going well."

Wilkinson is not a Method actor, but he did use Method techniques. It was not hard for him to imagine Valjean's sympathy for the downtrodden, nor his love for Cosette. As he played the role, he remembered the children and the wife he was to bring with him to America when he took his Valjean to Broadway. "In London I was missing them badly and was emotionally very sensitive," he said. "I'd be thinking of them as I sat down to sing 'Take Me Now'."

Yet this Valjean was not an ethereal figure, far from it. Wilkinson never shed the sense of danger that marked his performance at the show's start. He radiated physical as well as emotional strength, as all Valjeans must. The role is as taxing to the body as it is to the psyche. Wilkinson found singing for over two hours eight times a week tough on his throat and carrying Marius through those Paris sewers even tougher on his back, especially (he jokes) as Michael Ball, who created that role, had a taste for pizzas. At the Palace, he suffered a cracked rib, forcing him offstage for two weeks, and was warned by an osteopath that he could end up in a wheelchair. An operation on his back followed, leaving him with nothing worse than wear and tear.

Many remarkable men have now played Valjean, from Alfie Boe, a fan of the show since he heard the music at the age of 12 and who relished the challenge of mastering the character's "animalistic quality mixed with passion for justice", to the Australian pop singer and Vietnam veteran Normie Rowe, who has said he strongly identified with such an emotionally scarred person. Then there was the Israeli singer David "Dudu" Fisher. Described by Zubin Mehta as one of the five best tenors in the world, he has played the role in Tel Aviv, on Broadway and in London, singing "One Day More" at a Royal Variety Performance before the Queen and "Bring Him Home" to Pope Benedict XVI in Jerusalem.

Fisher, then becoming known as a cantor in Israel, had never heard of the musical when he came to London in 1987. His cousin, with whom he was staying, played him a cassette of the show, which so impressed him he went to the Palace Theatre to see it. "And I'll never forget it. I was sitting in row F, seat number 3, and I was crying all through the show and at the end I couldn't get up from my seat. Then I felt somebody tapping my shoulder, saying, 'Excuse me, sir, the show is over', and I said, 'No, sir, the show is just beginning'."

Above: Israeli cantor David "DuDu" Fisher premiered the role of Valjean in Tel Aviv in 1987 and subsequently appeared on Broadway and in London.

Right: Mitsuo Yoshihara (Valjean) and Takuya Kon (Javert), Tokyo, Japan, 2011.

Below, right: Daniel Koek made his West End debut as Valjean in 2013.

Indeed it was. Back home, Fisher learned from his manager that the Hebrew version of the show was soon to open in Tel Aviv and said, "What are you waiting for? Get me an audition." Even though he was known for singing liturgical music, had never had an acting lesson and had done little onstage save the occasional concert and Valjean was scheduled to be played by a famous Israeli performer, Fisher's rendition of "Bring Him Home" so impressed the director, the late Steven Pimlott, that he was cast in the role.

It is a sign of his success that Fisher, an observing Jew, was permitted to take off Friday nights and Saturday matinées when he appeared on Broadway, even though a second Valjean had to be hired. But his religious beliefs and his experience of singing in synagogues were creative strengths. Fisher felt a kinship with the character: "I wish I could be more like Valjean in my life, he was so caring for others. But then I was not Dudu Fisher when I was onstage. The character takes you over with its power and its beauty. I know that God was standing over Boublil and Schönberg when they wrote the piece. There's no doubt in my mind about that."

And still they come, Valjeans of every nationality. In 2012 the character was being played in the West End by Geronimo Rauch, a 34-year-old Argentine who had understudied Marius in Buenos Aires when he was 22 before triumphing as Valjean ten years later in Madrid in 2010. A video of him singing in English proved that he could handle that language as well as Spanish, and, in June 2012, he started a year's stint in London. The following year the Australian Daniel Koek became one of the youngest to play Valjean which remarkably was his first West End role. Recently Killian Donnelly, an Irishman, like the original Valjean Colm Wilkinson, has made the role his own having worked his way up through the ranks of the ensemble to become a star of musical theatre.

Left: Killian Donnelly as Valjean, London, 2017. Donnelly began as a swing in *Les Mis* in 2008, and over the next three years was promoted to cover Enjolras and Javert, before becoming principal Enjolras in 2010. He made a triumphant return to *Les Mis* in 2017 to play Valjean in London and on an international tour.

Right: Fifteen of the 17 Valjeans who took part in the finale of the Tenth Anniversary Concert at the Royal Albert Hall, London in October 1995. Back row: Jan Ježek, Jerzy Jeske, Takeshi Kaga, Gyula Vikidál. Middle row: Henk Poort, Reinhard Brussman, Craig Schulman, Kszysztof Stasierowski, Rob Guest, Tommy Körberg, Øystein Wiik, Kurt Ravn. Bottom row: Robert Marien, Michael Burgess and Egill Ólafsson.

Below: Shoichi Fukui has played Valjean in both the 25th and 30th Anniversary Japanese tours.

Bottom: Randall Keith regularly appeared as Valjean on the US Tour between 1999 and 2006.

Below, right: Geronimo Rauch who understudied Marius in Buenos Aires in 2000 and went on to play Valjean in Madrid in 2010 and in London in 2012-13.

CHAPTER 7

Inspector Javert

If the convict who broke his parole is the hero of *Les Misérables*, does it follow that the policeman obsessed with returning him to the chain gang is the villain? It would be hard to find anyone who has played Javert agreeing. John Diedrich, who performed him in Australia, was surely right to say that "the great mistake an actor might make is thinking him a bad man. He's not. He's a good man, a decent man, but he comes from a very hard society and is very, very hard". Trevor Nunn concurred: "He believes he's doing God's work on Earth, eradicating evil. He's passionate in his religion."

Still, it is also undeniable that his hardness and his passion become destructive and, in the end, self-destructive. Hugo himself compared the policeman to the whelp in the wolf-litter killed by his mother before it grows up and devours the rest of her young. Terrence Mann, who created the role on Broadway, cites that very passage – and also sees the character as a shark that moves silently through the water and then suddenly, terrifyingly strikes.

Yet Mann knows he is more complex, as did Hugo himself. Javert is as much the victim of his background as is the "criminal" who once felt impelled to steal bread to feed his nephew. He was born in prison himself, the son of a fortune-teller whose husband was in the galleys. He developed a consuming hatred of the vagabond class to which he then belonged, and reacted against it as fully as he could, carrying respect for authority to extremes. He is morality at its most punitive and cannot comprehend the merciful, forgiving morality of Jean Valjean.

The first Javert in the musical was Roger Allam, then a rising star with the RSC and now a fine classical actor and a three-times Olivier Award-winner. He had musical training, and even contemplated a career in opera, but was unsure whether to risk interrupting his theatre career by auditioning for the role. Nunn and Caird persuaded him to do so, as did a film of *Les Misérables* which, thanks to Charles Laughton's playing of the role, "seemed to be all about Javert". The result was a performance that the *Guardian*'s Michael Billington, no great friend of the show, felt brought "a haunted rectitude" and "depth" to the proceedings.

It is, Allam said, a "terrific part", allowing him to bring to life a man who could easily have followed his father by becoming a criminal: "I was very exercised by that. He'd changed, and the way he'd changed was to force himself into this straitjacket of moral rectitude. But what's appealing about the part is that here's someone who is fixed in a hard, stern view of the world that's cracked, fragmented, destroyed by seeing that Valjean has become a truly good man, almost a saint." Allam would have liked there to have been more meaty moral exchanges between Javert and Valjean, but

Above: Philip Quast is an outstanding Javert who has performed the role in the UK and Australia as well as at the tenth Anniversary Concert at the Royal Albert Hall in October 1995.

Opposite, above: Roger Allam as Javert with David Burt as Enjolras and assorted other cast members in rehearsals for the original London production in 1985.

Opposite, below left: The original Broadway cast featuring Terrence Mann as Javert and Braden Danner as Gavroche, 1987.

Opposite, below right: Since 1988 Michael McCarthy has sung Javert all over the world.

such things are hard to insert into big musicals with rapidly moving plots, and he was content with the song he himself had suggested: "Stars", in which Javert declares that his "is the way of the Lord".

He is not the only Olivier Award-winner to have played the role. Philip Quast has been pronounced Best Actor in a Musical three times, though not for his Javert, which he played in Australia and at *Les Mis*'s tenth Anniversary Concert in the Royal Albert Hall. The son of a farmer, brought up "in the middle of nowhere", educated in a forbiddingly conventional one-teacher school, and a man who admits "having problems with authority", the Australian actor nevertheless felt an odd empathy with the conventional, authoritarian policeman: "Because he's doing what he thinks is absolutely right. That's what 'Stars' is all about. He's a guide, overlooking the world and controlling it for what he believes is its good."

Above: Will Swenson delivers an emphatic performance as Javert on Broadway, 2014.

Opposite, above left: Norbert Lamla, who played Javert in Austria and Germany in 1988.

Opposite, above centre: John Diedrich as Javert, Australia, 1988.

Opposite, above right: Jeremy Secomb, London, 2016.

Opposite, bottom: Alfie Boe as Valjean and Norm Lewis as Javert confront each other at The O2 25th Anniversary Concert, 2010.

Quast's original audition for *Les Mis* in 1987, actually for the role of Enjolras, was at first comically unpromising. As he remembered it, he could not hit the right note in "Do You Hear the People Sing?", said he was terribly sorry, tried again and cracked again. He was, he said, so embarrassed that he grabbed the music, and, uttering the odd four-letter word, told Schönberg and Mackintosh that if they wanted to know how high he could sing they should have given him scales – "and I turned fast, nastily and viciously, and as I left the room Cameron said, 'Javert!'."

Quast got the part and prepared conscientiously for it. He read the Bible right through, learned the Ten Commandments and the divine ordinances that follow them, and carved, painted, polished and added a leather strip to the baton that Javert always carries with him and which he, Quast, has taken around the world. The reward was a highly praised performance that galvanized his career and was clearly particularly effective at the point when the policeman, freed by Valjean, commits suicide. As Quast played the scene, there was no conscious decision to die. He quoted Hugo, who wrote that what was happening to Javert was like the derailing of a train. His whole belief system had been turned upside down. He should have been killed by the desperate man he had long hunted and he was not. Freedom, for him, meant living in Hell. Even the stars he trusted now seemed black and cold. His life had been for nothing. Filled with these thoughts, Quast found himself instinctively climbing over the bridge to a death in the Seine that he saw as terribly ironic: "He'd lived a priest-like existence, and he's committing a Catholic country's greatest sin. It's like a Catholic priest killing himself."

As for Terrence Mann, he came to the role in an even stranger way than Quast. Appearing in a not-very-successful Broadway musical called *Rags* in 1986, he discovered that *Les Mis* was coming to New York. He then heard the British soundtrack: "And I remember listening to the role of Javert and thinking this is something I need to do. I was completely driven, to the point where I called my agent and tried and tried to get an audition."

That was denied him. But then he ran into a casting director, who suggested he audition for the role of Enjolras, leader of the rebel students. He did so, but decided to face Nunn, Boublil and Schönberg severely dressed in black, pulling back what was then long, black hair to emphasize his resemblance to Javert – "And as I was performing my song I saw Claude-Michel scrunch up his face and lean over to Trevor and mouth 'Enjolras? No, he's Javert'."

It was a triumphant ruse. Mann played the role for a year on Broadway, repeating it for the three months that ended *Les Mis*'s original run there in 2003 and winning a Tony® nomination for his powerful playing of a character he felt was no straightforward villain. Mann comes from America's southern Bible-belt and understood what it was to believe in a God of fear rather than a God of love. Living in New York in the 1970s, he found himself asking, perhaps like the young Javert, whether he himself was more cop or more criminal. As he agreed, his performance drew on something dangerous in himself: "Everybody's got the dark as well as the light. I was teetering on the edge a little bit. It cost some people their lives or their careers. I could have gone the wrong way, too"

Playing Javert's suicide eight times a week was, he says, pretty draining. It was clearly also shattering for his audiences. "Valjean's moment of compassion for him breaks into the depths of who Javert is. It breaks him apart. It's like a volcano coming from the centre of the Earth and spewing off its top. That's what happens when Javert jumps. That's where I got to every night." That's what New York unforgettably saw.

CHAPTER 8

Thénardier, Fantine & Significant Others

It's often said that *Les Misérables* is a show without stars or, rather, that the show itself is the star. And certainly Valjean and Javert are far from its only significant characters. Imagine *Les Mis* without Thénardier, the corrupt innkeeper who provides comic relief while embodying a parasitism that cannot be ignored and, thus, a more complete view of the human species than those two God-fearing men can offer. Imagine it without Marius, who grows from a lovelorn boy into an idealistic fighter, bringing romance to the show. Imagine it without Fantine, whose sickness and death bring Valjean his adopted daughter, Cosette – and depth and texture to the musical itself.

Indeed, you cannot imagine the show without several other characters, many of whom have been played by performers who have gone on to build impressive careers. In 2002, the Iranian-born Canadian actor Ramin Karimloo played the working-class rebel Feuilly in London's West End, understudying Marius and the rebel leader Enjolras; in 2004, he took over the role of Enjolras, reprising it in the 25th Anniversary Concert of *Les Misérables* in London's O2 Arena; he then played the title character in Andrew Lloyd Webber's *The Phantom of the Opera* and its sequel, *Love Never Dies*; and in 2011 he returned to the Queen's as a thrilling Valjean, a role he subsequently played in Canada and in which he made his Broadway debut in 2014. Another highly successful Enjolras, the Australian Anthony Warlow, has also gone on to play many leading roles in the years since, including the Phantom.

And what of Thénardier's tragic daughter, Eponine? That role won a Tony® Award for Frances Ruffelle, who performed it in the original London and New York productions and it has proved a launch pad for many others. The Filipino singer and actress Lea Salonga sang "On My Own" when she auditioned for the part of Kim in *Miss Saigon* and she later played Eponine in the Broadway and West End productions and on tour in America. The role of Cosette has also been a platform for stars of the future: Ashley Tisdale, who was to star in Disney's *High School Musical*, played Little Cosette in America, while Judy Kuhn, who took the role of the grown-up Cosette in the original Broadway production and was nominated for a Tony®, went on to a very successful career in musical theatre with many other nominations to her credit. The role of Gavroche has also launched successful performers, among them the pop singer Nick Jonas, who played the boy on Broadway in 2003 and, seven years later,

Opposite: Ramin Karimloo as Enjolras and Ian Sharp as Joly, London, 2004.

Above: Patti LuPone as Fantine singing "I Dreamed a Dream" in the original London production in 1985.

Above: The cast of *Les Misérables* featuring Phil Daniels as Thénardier, London, 2015.

Opposite, left above: Samantha Barks as Eponine and Alistair Brammer as Marius perform "A Little Fall of Rain", London, 2010.

Opposite, left below: Rachelle Ann Go played Fantine in London in 2015-2016 and returned to her native Philippines to sing the role in the Australian/Asian tour in 2016.

Opposite, right: Frances Ruffelle as Eponine singing "A Heart Full of Love", 1985.

Marius in both the West End and that O2 concert. You might say that *Les Mis* has acted as a career catalyst.

However, the original Fantine was already a star. The American actress Patti LuPone had won the first of several Tony® Awards for her playing of the title-character in Andrew Lloyd Webber's *Evita*, and had impressed Mackintosh as Nancy in his Broadway production of *Oliver!* in 1984. The next year, he came to her New York apartment and played her the cassette of the French *Les Mis*: "After four bars I went, 'Whoops, this is going to be huge, where are you staging it?' and he said, 'It's opening at the RSC,' and I said, 'This is never going to happen again so I'd be stupid not to say yes.'"

It was a happy encounter, for the creative team had not then been able to find an English performer able to handle all the role's musical and acting demands. Moreover, LuPone was actually in London as rehearsals for *Les Mis* began, giving an Olivier-winning performance in Marc Blitzstein's *The Cradle Will Rock*. Caird recalled her coming to meet the creative team, sitting by a piano, sight-reading part of Fantine's "I Dreamed a Dream": "It was game, set and match. She's one of the great voices and a great actress, too."

As LuPone said, Fantine is "the tragic element at the top of the show" and vital to the plot. But then she is offstage until she reappears as a ghost at the end. So when LuPone told Mackintosh that she would not be going on to Broadway when her West End stint ended, the producer thought it was because the role was too small for the Broadway star of *Evita*. "But I said it's because this has been the perfect theatrical experience: the perfect cast, the perfect environment, the RSC, and a very discerning audience. This is my experience, it will never be repeated, and I don't want it repeated. I want to have been a member of the original London company, over and out."

The original company also included Michael Ball, who is now a major star on both sides of the Atlantic and the winner of two Olivier Awards for an hilarious performance in *Hairspray* and as a brilliant Sweeney Todd, but back then was an unknown 23-year-old, discovered by Mackintosh when he went to Manchester to see him in a production of Gilbert and Sullivan's *The Pirates of Penzance*. Ball had already asked his then agent if he should audition for *Les Mis*, only to be told "There's nothing in it for you", but now he went to London, auditioned successfully, and became a notably fresh, vulnerable and intense Marius.

"It wasn't your typical juvenile lead," he explained. "He was a boy turning into a man. First, he falls in love with a girl in a street in the middle of Paris, and then he's prepared to sacrifice his life for his belief of

Above, left: Debbie Gibson made her début as Eponine, Broadway, 1992.

Above, right: Anthony Warlow as Enjolras and Simon Burke as Marius, Sydney, 1987.

Opposite, top: Matt Lucas as Thénardier, Craig Mather as Marius and Katy Secombe as Madame Thénardier, London, 2011.

Opposite, below: "One Day More", London, 2016.

what society should be. It's a rite of passage and a microcosm of every decent bloke's story."

A rite of passage for Ball, too, since *Les Mis* launched his career. However, he had serious problems when the show moved from the Barbican to the Palace. Glandular fever struck. He took six weeks off, but when he returned exhaustion escalated into ME: "I started having panic attacks. I got terrible stage fright. My body couldn't cope, that played on my mind, and I lost it. I was having a breakdown and had to leave the show." He could, he said, have left showbusiness altogether, but Mackintosh offered him the crucial role of Raoul when Lloyd Webber's *The Phantom of the Opera* was being recast – and he reprised Marius at the show's tenth anniversary show in the Albert Hall and played Valjean himself before the Queen at Windsor Castle in 2004.

Alun Armstrong, the first Thénardier, has also won an Olivier Award, in his case for Sweeney Todd in 1993. *Les Misérables* had been the favourite book of his father, a Durham coalminer, Methodist lay preacher and something of a singer. Though Alun himself had not read the novel, he knew all about "Gene Valgene", as his father called the hero.

Along with his awful wife, Thénardier is the villain, in Armstrong's words "foul, an absolute scumbag, but because he's wily he becomes comic. He fleeces all his customers with a nod, nod, wink, wink to the audience, as if to say this is what I do when they're not looking, and of course people laugh". The actor was put in mind of a London spiv, and at his audition sang "Master of the House", in which Thénardier boasts of cooking books and watering wine, in a Cockney accent. That is still what is heard in the West End *Les Mis*, as is the number that makes it clear that Thénardier is not just comic relief:

Above: Lea Salonga as Fantine, New York, 2007.

Right: Euan Doidge as Marius, Melbourne, 2014.

Below: Harry Jardine as Gavroche, London, 2003.

Opposite: Gary Beach as Thénardier and Gina Ferrall as Mme Thénardier, San Francisco, 1989.

"Dog Eats Dog", which was added so late that Armstrong had sung it only once ("terrifying but elating!") before the first preview.

Armstrong is one of the UK's most brilliantly versatile actors – his credits vary from the lead in Arthur Miller's *Death of a Salesman* at the National Theatre to many major television and film roles including Mornay in *Braveheart* – and a hard act for anyone to follow. But there have been many successful Thénardiers: among them Leo Burmester on Broadway, who saw him as "the kind of guy who will show you a great time, just to take your money, but when the chips are down, he'll kill you as soon as look as you"; William Zappa in Australia, for whom he was a man with the cynicism to make an audience laugh even while they are despising him, thus ensuring the show did not become "relentless misery"; and the British comic actor Matt Lucas.

Lucas had loved the show ever since his parents took him to see it as a 13th birthday present in 1987 and told Cameron Mackintosh so when the producer saw him in the stage version of the BBC television show *Little Britain* in 2005. The result was that he auditioned for Mackintosh, half-jokingly saying he would like to play Javert, but actually being cast as Thénardier for the show's 25th Anniversary Concert at the O2 arena and, later, in the West End. And he brought a memorably sly, sinister quality to the character, fitting his belief that the innkeeper is "dangerous and unpredictable – a psychopath basically".

There's the moral as well as the theatrical challenge for any actor tackling the role. "You have the license to be mischievous, to break out of the piece occasionally and wink at the audience," said Lucas. "But it becomes clear that the Thénardiers are not loveable rogues or rascals but really disgusting people, vile. That's not to say you can't have fun playing them, but it's important to catch the dark side, too." Nobody has put the case better.

CHAPTER 9

To America

The British reviews may have been disappointing, but those that appeared in the American papers after the show's Barbican opening were the very opposite. *Newsweek*'s Edward Behr wrote that *Les Mis* was "spectacular, enchanting, a believable, universally relevant tale provoking laughter, tears and the uplift of truly great theatre". *Time* magazine's William Henry III found the show "thrilling". In the *International Herald Tribune* Sheridan Morley praised the musical's energy, intensity and "blazing theatricality". And I (Benedict Nightingale), though shamefully underreacting to a score whose glory I recognized only later, gave it a rave review in the *New York Times.*

As Morley and others pointed out, the show was also genuinely groundbreaking. After all, sung-through musicals were virtually non-existent in the 1980s, as were shows that treated serious subjects for a popular audience. Moreover, it was surprising to find a Shakespearean company applying the lessons it had learned on productions from *Hamlet* to *Nicholas Nickleby* to a musical it hoped would flourish in the West End. And bringing to musical life an epic novel by as formidable a writer as Hugo was groundbreaking in itself.

That was particularly gratifying because some of the major American producers and directors had earlier expressed doubts and worse. Bernard Jacobs, president of the powerful Shubert Organization, told John Caird the show was going to be a downer, "and when you've got a stiff you bury it". Many people had to eat their words when the show transferred to Broadway, among them Gerald Schoenfeld, the Shubert chairman, who congratulated Cameron Mackintosh on having changed and rescued a dud show, only to be told that it was virtually identical to the show he had seen in London – just shorter!

The all-important American opening actually occurred in Washington in December 1986, by when it was clear that the show had become a mega-hit back home. In London *Les Mis* had not only sold out, but also it had paid back its investors within six months and yielded over £2.5 million in profits within a year. Could it do as well in America? A sold-out run lasting two months at the Kennedy Center gave the initial answer. The public in a city chosen largely because of its sophistication and political awareness agreed with the *Washington Post*'s David Richards, who hailed a musical that "unfurls all the great emotions – pride, pity, greed, compassion and love – and then waves them like banners on high".

Left: One of the eight Tony® Awards won by the show, June 1987.

Opposite, top left: An invitation to the party after the opening night on Broadway, 12 March 1987.

Opposite, top right: A ticket for the opening night of the New York production of Les Misérables at the Broadway Theatre, 12 March 1987.

Opposite, below left: Unlike the British press, *Newsweek*, *Time* magazine and the *New York Times* gave the show rave opening reviews.

Opposite far right: After opening at the Broadway Theatre on 12 March 1987, the show moved to the Imperial Theatre, New York, where it played until 2003.

Cameron Mackintosh
requests the pleasure of
your Company
at a Party
to be held at
THE ARMORY
Park Avenue at 67th Street
New York City
to celebrate
the Broadway opening of

Les Misérables

immediately following the performance
on Thursday March 12th, 1987

Admit One

Black Tie optional

BROADWAY THEATRE
1681 BROADWAY N.Y.C.
LES MISERABLES

6:00 P THU MAR 12 1987

22
01

$47.50
ORCH10
3
22
6:00 P
B 101

LOCATION

The Shubert Organization

From the brothel to the barricades: LuPone as a prostitute driven by desperation

Theater

A Jubilant Cry from the Gutter

LES MISERABLES *by Alain Boublil and Claude-Michel Schönberg*

Trevor Nunn has reached the shadow-boxing phase, the most perilous in any ... Having staged one of the ...

yet it provides hummable pop tunes. Like *Jesus Christ Superstar* and *Evita, Les Misérables* originated as a double-...

A Splendid 'Les Miserables'

Musicals are the riskiest gamble in show business. For every "Fiddler on the Roof" or "My Fair Lady," hundreds have sunk without a trace—except for the holes in ... time to ... makes h...

less and thoroughly credible performance. And then there is Colm Wilkinson (Valjean). An actor-singer of immense range, ... a tour de ... ensitive. ... is show. ... that is a

Stage: 'Misérables,' Opens on Broadway

By FRANK RICH

IF anyone doubts that the contemporary musical theater can flex its atrophied muscles and yank an audience right out of its seats, he need look no further than the Act I finale of "Les Misérables."

At that point in the gripping pop opera at the Broadway, the strands of narrative culled from Victor Hugo's novel of early-19th-century France in-...

The ensuing fusion of drama, music, character, design and movement is what links this English adaptation of a French show to the highest tradition of modern Broadway musical production. One can hardly watch the Act I finale without thinking of the star-crossed lovers and rival gangs preparing for the rumble in the "Tonight" quintet of "West Side Story" — or of the revolving-stage dispersal of Tevye's shtetl following the pogrom in "Fiddler on the Roof." In

He was praising a company that now was almost entirely American but still led by Colm Wilkinson. The creative team had sounded out home-grown performers for the role of Valjean, among them Mandy Patinkin, but had ended up persuading Actors' Equity that the Irishman was the man for the job. He and Frances Ruffelle, awarded the role of Eponine after an American actress pulled out, were the only members of the original company to repeat their roles across the Atlantic.

Altogether, it had taken time to assemble a cast that satisfied the creative team. Caird remembered trying to create an ensemble able to play the nineteenth-century French poor when all the chorus boys coming to the audition "looked like cowboys – broad shoulders, slim waists, good teeth – when we needed the weird ones, the funny ones, the balding ones, the slightly overweight ones". And many of those who did join the company, and were used to imperious musical-theatre directors, were clearly surprised to find rehearsals proceeding along RSC lines.

"They love actors," Terrence Mann said of Nunn and Caird. "Nobody shouted or yelled. It was such a respectful, dignified process, the whole atmosphere was practically sacred and it brought out the best in everybody." All took part in many of the same bonding exercises and imaginative improvisations that had occurred in London. Performers invented names and background stories for minimal characters, one actress deciding that the beggar she was playing was called Hedy La Marc and had been abandoned, pregnant and syphilitic, by her lover. But there were also differences, as when they sat in a large circle and, one by one, confided how their forebears came to America, often to escape the same injustice, poverty and degradation that afflicted Hugo's characters. "Suddenly everybody was an RSC actor," recalled Richard Jay-Alexander, the American associate director, "they were no longer frivolous musical people running around in dance shoes."

It worked, triumphantly. By the time of its New York opening in March 1987, a production that had cost $4.5 million to mount had made a profit of $1 million in Washington and, thanks to great out-of-town word of mouth, could boast a record $12-million advance at the Broadway Theatre. Indeed, the show had taken a then astonishing $447,274 on the first day that tickets had gone on sale in New York. And the first night on Broadway brought an ecstatic ovation, followed by a party packed with celebrities, among them Raquel Welch, Calvin Klein and Mayor Koch, who said the show was "superb, everything I expected and more". Then came the verdicts from the reviewers. The *New York Post*'s Clive Barnes found the show "simply smashing – every expectation is fulfilled" and the *New York Times*'s influential Frank Rich lauded a "gripping" musical that could "yank an audience right out of its seats", reserving special praise for Ruffelle's "stunning" Eponine and Wilkinson's Valjean, who was "convincingly brawny, Christlike without being cloying, enraged by injustice, paternal with children".

Les Misérables had done poorly in London's Olivier Awards, losing to the revival of a 1930s musical *Me and My Girl*, though Patti LuPone's Fantine was cited along with her performance in *The Cradle Will Rock* when she was named Best Actress in a Musical. But it swept the Tonys®, winning eight awards in all, including ones for Napier, Ruffelle and Schönberg, who wryly thanked Puccini for not having completed his version of *Les Misérables*. And it became the second longest-running show in Broadway history early in 2002, having played for 6,138 performances, first at the Broadway Theatre, then at the Imperial. "There's life in the old girl yet," declared a jubilant Cameron Mackintosh as he came onstage, adding his thanks to Victor Hugo, "200 years old next month", for "never charging me any royalties".

There would probably have been even more life in the old girl but for 9/11, which was widely blamed for keeping tourists away from New York

Opposite: Kyle Scatliffe (Enjolras) rallies the students on the barricade, New York, 2014.

Above, left: Gaten Matarazzo, young star of *Stranger Things*, as Gavroche in New York, 2014.

Above, top right: A seasonally themed *Les Mis* mouse mat produced to promote the show's run at the Imperial Theatre, New York, 2014.

Above, right: Andy Mientus as Marius and Samantha Hill as Cosette in New York, 2014.

and causing the first Broadway production's closure in May 2003. It was a success that Mackintosh told that 2002 audience he "never, ever dreamed would happen", but one that was not without incident. Mackintosh is a hands-on impresario, one who keeps a personal eye on all his productions and strives to keep them fresh. However, American Equity's rules meant that it was virtually impossible to replace ensemble performers, with the result that, Mackintosh recalled, "we had 40- or 50-year-old students climbing up the barricades with their bus passes". A stand-off was ended in 1997, but only by closing the original Broadway production, replacing it for five weeks with a touring version of *Les Mis*, rehearsing a substantially new company and, after giving substantial payoffs to those made redundant, opening again.

Meanwhile, three different touring companies had flourished in the United States, as had one production in Canada, meaning that at one time five stagings of *Les Mis* were simultaneously available in North America. While one of these was ensconced in major Eastern or mid-Western cities, from Boston to Chicago, another encamped in the West, and the third usually played single weeks in such places as East Lansing, Michigan, visiting a total of more than 150 cities, some several times, during its almost 18-year existence. All the US companies of this period were staged by Richard Jay-Alexander, who remains convinced that *Les Mis* is the "greatest musical of all time".

For him, the only obvious difference between the British and American productions of the show came when low-life characters were required, for

Music up: "One Day More"

Les Misérables

Paris 1832

Paris 1832

A revolution!

Voice over: LES MISÉRABLES. Newsweek calls it "a musical that makes history!"

Visual: TITLE bleeds through to "Paris 1832" which ignites, burnt through by WIDE SHOT of entire company at barricade.

Waged by men ... endured by women... fired by passion, but filled with hate --

CUT TO MCU of men DISSOLVE SLOWLY to women... DOLLY 360° around Marius/Cosette – they "turn into" Javert and Valjean

From the mean in spirit, to the pure of heart - it swept into every corner and forever changed the face of a

CUT TO Thénardier and "Master of the House" scene

CUT TO Fantine - push into her "thoughts"

DISSOLVE to little Cosette alone on stage - wide shot. Push in on her face and DISSOLVE (MATCH) to art.

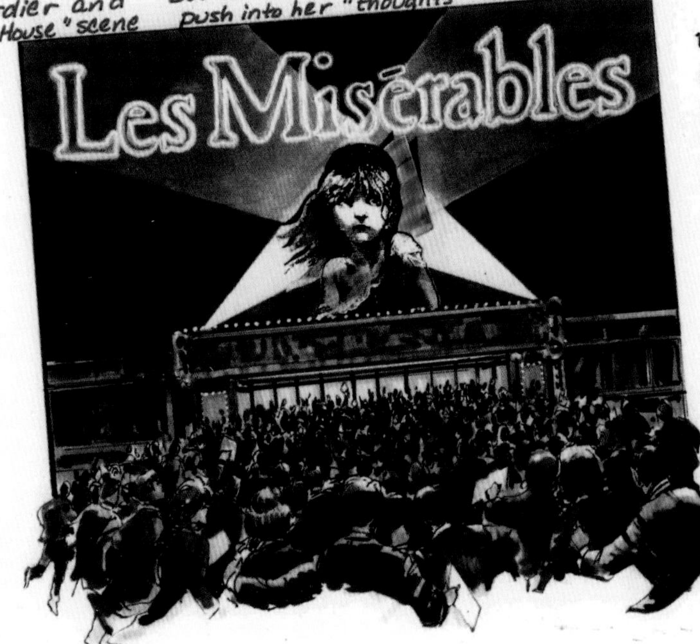

nation!

LES MISÉRABLES.

When the beating of your heart echoes the beating of the drum... the revolution has come to Broadway.

FIGHT TO GET A TICKET!

Pull back and crane up to discover "all of London" storming the Palace Theatre.

The revolution on stage has inspired a theatrical revolution unparralled. The crowd is indeed all but ready to "fight to get a ticket."

instance in Thénardier's inn. In London a class divide was evident from the Cockney accents, but the USA is filled with regional accents that do not denote such distinctions, encouraging him to opt for performers who were "rough and tumble, a little raw".

He sees it as a nursery for performers, many of whom have gone on from *Les Mis* to have successful musical careers. The actress and singer Lea Michele, one of the stars of the TV series *Glee*, whom he remembered as a bright eight-year-old from the Bronx when she played the young Cosette on Broadway in 1995, returned to take the role of Eponine at his Hollywood Bowl staging of *Les Mis* in 2008. An earlier young Cosette, Lacey Chabert, went on to star in *Mean Girls* and other films. Ricky Martin became Broadway's Marius in 1996 and is now one of the world's best-known pop singers and musical actors. Anthony Crivello, a member of the original ensemble, won a Tony® award for his performance in *Kiss of the Spider Woman*. Aged just 21, the singer Debbie Gibson made her Broadway debut as Eponine in 1992.

The alumni list grows, as did *Les Mis* itself, everywhere helped by clever marketing. Everyone must now recognize the logo taken from an etching of Cosette by Hugo's favourite illustrator, Emile Bayard. The forlorn little girl with the big broomstick has been adapted to suit place after place in America, meaning that she has often worn the shirt of a local football team. In Philadelphia, she hung upside down from the city's Liberty Bell, in Los Angeles sported dark glasses, and in New York multiplied into a parody of Andy Warhol's coloured faces of Marilyn Monroe. "Those tweaks gave the impression we weren't the same old show that had played last week in Milwaukee or Peoria," said Alan Wasser, Mackintosh's North American general manager.

But then Mackintosh's teams have always been proactive when it comes to selling the show, preparing audiences in large American cities with radio ads far in advance of its opening, placing the Cosette logo on buses, sending press packages to college newspapers, getting department stores to set up *Les Mis* displays, or, in smaller places, giving free tickets to hairdressers, taxi-drivers and others likely to spread news of its advent. Though not for commercial reasons, the touring companies have also made friends by contributing to local charities, and not only to the poor, homeless and "miserables". Cast members set aside earnings for the victims of the Oklahoma City bombing in 1995 and, unforgettably, for those injured or displaced by the devastating San Francisco earthquake of 1989.

That event showed what *Les Mis* can achieve. The theatre next to the Curran, where the show was about to open, was wrecked, but the Curran itself had no structural damage. Still, nobody could be sure if shocked spectators would come to *Les Mis*'s first preview. But they did, and, as Jay-Alexander recalled, the experience was "really, really overwhelming – the ovation must have gone on for six-and-a-half minutes. Our blood was in that performance, our guts were there, our love was there. It was the most emotional thing I'd ever experienced and as the paper said on its front page the next day, it was healing for San Francisco."

Left: Cosette hanging from Philadelphia's Liberty Bell.

Opposite: A storyboard for a proposed television advertising campaign prior to the Broadway opening, 1987.

Above, left to right: Colm Wilkinson as Valjean, Judy Kuhn as Cosette and Randy Graff as Fantine were members of the original cast on Broadway, 1987; Lea Michele, star of the popular American television series *Glee*, made her Broadway debut as Young Cosette in 1995; After a successful career in a boy band and as a solo artist, the Puerto Rican star Ricky Martin achieved a lifetime's ambition by appearing as Marius on Broadway in 1996.

Following pages: The barricade scene, US second national tour in Toronto, 1989.

CHAPTER 10

Les Misérables Goes Global

By the tenth anniversary of its Barbican opening, *Les Mis* had been in production in over 140 cities worldwide. But as Boublil and Schönberg said years ago, "America, Paris or London, what's the difference? The heart reacts the same way everywhere". As David "DuDu" Fisher, put it, "In every country you find the same problems, the same poverty, the same tragedy, the same injustice" – and, he might have added, the same hankering for redemption, reconciliation and love.

Yet Fisher found himself thinking of young Israeli soldiers in what was virtually a war zone around their own country, when he sang "Bring Him Home" with particular fervour and reckoned the song would also have a special resonance in nations that have sent sons to Afghanistan. The message of *Les Mis*, though universal, can also seem strikingly specific.

So it certainly was when the show appeared in an Eastern Europe about to shed its communist shackles. There was what Jennifer Till, then Mackintosh's head of licensing, remembers as a wonderful production in 1988 in Gdynia, in Poland. An impoverished company had saved up foreign currency for years to pay for the radio mikes they needed to make it musically excellent. The production was simply staged, even rough-edged, yet almost the stronger for that. The lead actor was short, stocky, muscular, and, said Till, really looked as if he had been breaking stones. Since the Catholic Church was prominent in the battle for freedom, and the Solidarity-supporting priest, Father Jerzy Popieluszko, had recently been murdered, there was extra power to Valjean's dying words, "to love another person is to see the face of God".

The Polish actors playing the students refused to flourish a red flag on barricades that consisted of a jumble of chairs and tables, insisting on a

Above: A ticket for the Stadsschouwburg Theater, Antwerp, Belgium, 1998.

Right: Talia del Val as Cosette, Spanish tour, 2013.

Top: The Raimund Theater, Vienna, Austria, 15 September 1988.

Above: The Musical Theater, Duisburg, Germany, 1996.

Left: A gala première ticket for the Theater des Westens, Berlin, Germany, 2003.

Polish one instead. And before the closing "Do You Hear the People Sing?" the cast used the Solidarity salute, an upturned fist. "It was," said Till, "pin-drop time."

The Bishop's line to Valjean, "I have bought your soul for God", clearly resonated in many places; for instance, in the city of Szeged, where a production was staged in front of the enormous Votive Church of Our Lady of Hungary, a nation that had suffered street fighting and seen its aspiring democrats defeated back in 1956. In Prague, whose people still brought nightly candles to the spot in Wenceslas Square where the student Jan Palach had incinerated himself, the murdered students of *Les Mis* didn't remain at the back while Marius sang "Empty Chairs at Empty Tables"; they walked forward, each placing a candle on the stage.

Some foreign productions have been "reproductions", meaning that a creative team from London, New York or Australia would replicate the original staging with indigenous talent. But more than half the overseas productions are "local", presented by local managements who must convince Cameron Mackintosh that they fully understand the complexity of the production and are able to put together the best creative talent in their country. Mackintosh personally vets the translation, approves the entire creative team and their designs as well as their principal casting. If things went awry, Till said her main weapon was to say "Cameron wouldn't like it", and the show would usually improve.

There has been the odd failure, for instance in *Les Mis*'s home town of Paris, where a French-language production lost two million francs, because apart from a hard core of musical theatergoers who can only fill a theatre for three or four months, in Nick Allott's view too many people "like operetta and grand opera but have no real regard for musical theatre". But mostly there have been major successes, as in Oslo, where at least 10 per cent of the population, many more than once, saw the first of several Norwegian productions, or Copenhagen where the show was presented in the former gasworks and the local producers were astonished by uncharacteristically long ovations. São Paulo was also a success. Even though Cameron Mackintosh arrived just before the opening to find only ten tickets sold, it actually went on to run for almost two years. There are cities where booking in advance is not the tradition.

Nunn himself went to Australia to stage the production that opened in Sydney in 1987, initially with Normie Rowe as Valjean and Deborah Byrne as Fantine. According to Philip Quast, its Javert, this had a powerful impact in a country which had been a penal colony – "a place where people were sent because others believed that, like Valjean, they were born bad, but where they got freed, bred and became landowners".

Above, left: Carrie Hope Fletcher reprised the role of Eponine in the Dubai première of *Les Mis*, 2016.

Above, right: Clockwise from the left, Natalie Mendoza (Eponine), Dave Willetts (Valjean), Rachael Beck (Fantine) Theresa Borg (Cosette) and David Campbell (Marius) in Sydney, Australia, 1997.

Right: A poster advertising *Les Misérables* at the Teatr Muzyczny in Gydnia, Poland, in 1989.

Below: An advertisement in the UK press announcing the. Australian premiere, 1987.

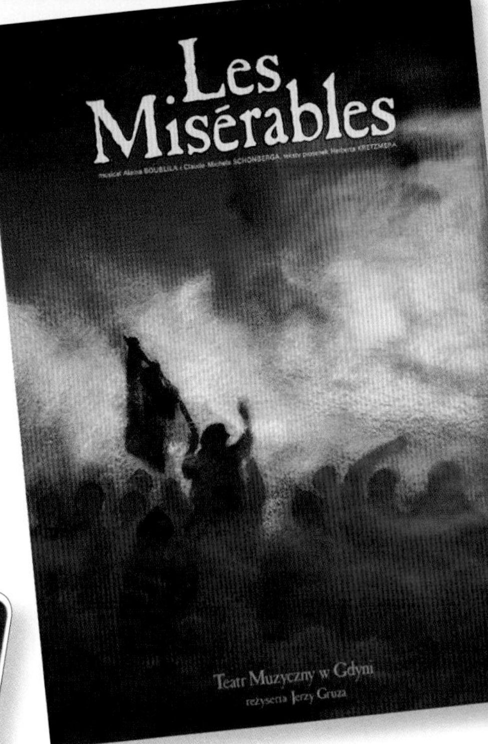

Above, left: Richard Carlsohn as Marius and Liv Ragnhild Somme as Cosette singing "A Heart Full of Love", Norway, 1988.

Top, right: Emily Bautista as Eponine, US tour, 2018.

Right: The Guinness World Records certificate awarded to *Les Misérables* in 2005.

CERTIFICATE

Since first opening on 8 October 1985, Sir Cameron Mackintosh's production of Les Misérables has had a record 15 productions staged around the world at one time, with 11 (nine resident and two tours) playing as of February 2005.

Keeper of the Records
GUINNESS WORLD RECORDS LTD

With an upside-down Cosette as its logo, the production played in Australia's main cities, and closed in Auckland, New Zealand, after 1,337 performances. A tenth-anniversary *Les Mis* toured the Antipodes for two years between 1997 and 1999 – "doing great business," according to John Robertson, Mackintosh's executive producer – and yet another Australian staging went to Singapore, Cape Town, Hong Kong and Seoul.

The East has been notably hospitable to the show. Mainland China has seen it in Shanghai while Korea first hosted an English language production as part of an Asian/South African tour in 1996, the subsequent two productions have been produced locally and have played triumphantly in the Korean language.

In Japan it has run up thousands of performances over 31 years. John Caird staged the first production at Tokyo's Imperial Theatre in 1987. There were problems with translation, since Japanese is a language in which every syllable must contain a vowel and the script took up too much space to be easily fitted into Schönberg's music. Two famous leading actors, Takeshi Kaga and Sakae Takita, alternated the role of Valjean. And, subsequently, all the main characters have had anything between two and four performers alternating them. It was hard for Caird to give notes to one Marius or Javert when three others were crowding around him.

Les Mis has already become Japan's most popular musical ever and in 2017 celebrated the 30th anniversary of its original opening in Tokyo. Not that Caird initially believed in the evidence of that success, since Japanese audiences stay quiet during the show itself. "I got really worried at first," he said. "The pressure was intense with the royal family due to come to a lavish opening … throughout the show there were only tiny ripples of applause. But even at the first preview the applause at the end went on and on. I was used to the Broadway standing ovation, which lasts a minute while people are putting on their coats. But here there were five, ten, twenty curtain calls. We actually had to stop them clapping and make them go home."

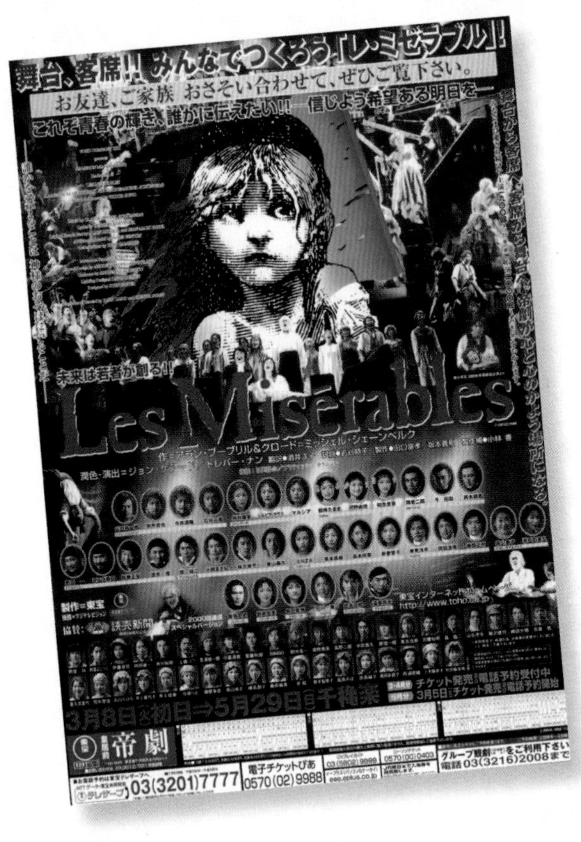

Left: A leaflet promoting *Les Misérables* at the Imperial Theatre, Tokyo in spring 2005.

Right: Carly Rose Sonenclar as Little Cosette, New York, 2007.

Below, right: A *Les Misérables* brochure, Daegu, Korea, November 2012.

Below: The finale of the Japanese production of *Les Misérables*, Tokyo, 2011.

The Chinese have so far seen only an English-language production that brought a US company supplemented by international principals including Colm Wilkinson as Valjean from San Francisco to Shanghai in 2002. Nick Allott recalled the opening night of a three-week run, with many of the seats filled by party notables. "I thought we were dying a death. There was no reaction to any of the songs, but when the students picked up the red flag in the ABC café at the end of act one, there was an audible gasp, and I felt 'we've connected, we've really connected', and from that moment the show went whoosh."

Right, top: An enthusiastic press cutting from the *China Daily* newspaper.

Right, below: A leaflet for the Grand Theatre, Shanghai, 2002. Colm Wilkinson and Michael McCarthy led a company who were mostly from the US tour in a three-week engagement presenting the first full production of a Western musical in China.

Below: Advertisement announcing the Shanghai premiere in *The New York Times*, 21 June 2002.

CHINA DAILY

ARTS & CULTURE

Original 'Les Mis' captures Shanghai

'Emperor of Musicals' quenches local audience with classic

Les Misérables The Original and 25th Anniversary Productions Around the World

MANCHESTER

LONDON

Since 1985 *Les Misérables* has been performed in a fully staged or concert version in 422 cities in 51 countries. It has made more than one visit to 175 of those cities and an extraordinary six or more visits to 40 cities in the United States. Cleveland, St Louis and St Paul compete for the record with 11 visits each. Space precludes us listing more than 150 additional US and Canadian productions licensed by Music Theatre International since 2007.

Les Misérables has travelled the world from Australia to Canada from South America to Japan, where it has been seen in Tokyo 18 times. The islands of Mauritius, Bermuda and the Dominican Republic have all played host to the show. In 1989 the show was playing somewhere in the world 24 hours a day. The fourth UK Tour opens in late 2018, meanwhile bookings for the fifth American tour stretch well into 2019, proving the show's enduring global appeal.

BROADWAY

MEXICO CITY

BRAZIL

LOS ANGELES

DUBAI

London, Barbican Theatre
30.09.85 - 23.11.85

London, Palace Theatre
04.12.85 - 27.03.04

London, Queen's Theatre
03.04.04 – to date

UK TOURS 1 & 2
Plymouth
Birmingham (twice)
Manchester (3 times)
Bristol (twice)
Southampton
Bradford
Edinburgh (twice)
Liverpool
Dublin (twice)
Sheffield
Newcastle

UK 25th ANNIVERSARY TOUR
Cardiff
Manchester
Norwich
Birmingham
Edinburgh
Paris
Bristol
Salford
Southampton
London, Barbican Theatre

UK TOUR 4
Leicester, The Curve
Opens 14.11.18

USA
Washington, Kennedy Center
27.12.86 - 14.02.87
New York, Broadway Theatre
12.03.87 - 13.10.90
New York, Imperial Theatre
17.10.90 - 18.05.03
New York, Broadhurst Theatre
21.10.06 - 06.01.08
New York, Imperial Theatre
01.03.14 - 04.09.16

US TOURS 1 & 2
Boston (twice)
Washington (twice)
Philadelphia (twice)
Chicago (twice)
Detroit
Baltimore
Los Angeles (twice)
San Francisco

US TOURS 3 & 4
Akron
Albuquerque (4 times)
Amarillo
Appleton
Atlanta (9 times)
Augusta
Austin (4 times)
Bakersfield (twice)
Baltimore (7 times)
Baton Rouge
Birmingham (4 times)
Bloomington (3 times)
Boise (3 times)
Boston (7 times)
Buffalo (7 times)
Calgary* (3 times)
Champaign (3 times)
Charleston (3 times)
Charlotte (7 times)
Chattanooga (twice)
Chicago (6 times)
Cincinnati (9 times)
Clearwater (twice)
Cleveland (11 times)
College Station
Colorado Springs
Columbia (twice)
Columbus (8 times)
Corpus Christi
Costa Mesa (4 times)
Cupertino (twice)
Dallas (7 times)
Dayton (5 times)
Denver (10 times)
Des Moines (7 times)
Detroit (9 times)
Duluth
East Lansing (6 times)
Edmonton* (3 times)
El Paso (twice)
Escondido
Eugene (twice)
Evansville (twice)
Fayetteville (twice)
Flint
Fort Lauderdale (3 times)
Fort Myers (4 times)
Fort Wayne (twice)
Fort Worth (7 times)
Fresno (3 times)
Gainesville (twice)
Grand Rapids (5 times)
Green Bay (4 times)
Greensboro (twice)
Greenville (5 times)
Hartford (6 times)
Hershey (4 times)
Honolulu
Houston (7 times)
Huntsville (3 times)
Indianapolis (7 times)
Iowa City (5 times)
Jackson
Jacksonville (5 times)
Kalamazoo (4 times)
Kansas City (8 times)
Kitchener* (twice)
Knoxville (5 times)
Las Vegas (6 times)
Lincoln (4 times)
Little Rock (3 times)
Long Beach (twice)
Los Angeles (5 times)
Louisville (7 times)
Lubbock (3 times)
Madison (4 times)
Melbourne (twice)
Memphis (8 times)
Miami
Miami Beach (5 times)
Milwaukee (6 times)
Minneapolis (twice)
Mobile (twice)
Montreal*
Muncie
Myrtle Beach (twice)
Nashville (7 times)
Naples
New Haven (4 times)
New Jersey
New Orleans (5 times)
Newark
Norfolk (4 times)
Oklahoma (4 times)
Omaha (4 times)
Orlando (7 times)
Ottawa* (twice)
Palm Desert
Pasadena (twice)
Peoria (4 times)
Philadelphia (8 times)
Phoenix
Pittsburgh (9 times)
Portland (6 times)
Portsmouth
Providence (7 times)
Raleigh (7 times)
Rapid City
Regina (twice)
Reno (twice)
Richmond (5 times)
Roanoke (twice)
Rochester (7 times)
Rockford
Sacramento (6 times)
Saginaw
Salt Lake City (9 times)
San Antonio (5 times)
San Diego (6 times)
San Francisco (5 times)
San Jose (3 times)
Sarasota (twice)
Saskatoon* (twice)
Savannah
Schenectady (5 times)
Scranton (3 times)
Seattle (9 times)
Shreveport
Sioux City
South Bend
Spokane (5 times)
Springfield, Missouri (twice)
Springfield, Illinois (3 times)
St Louis, (11 times)
St Paul (11 times)
St Petersburg
State College (twice)
Syracuse (5 times)
Tallahassee
Tampa (7 times)
Tempe (9 times)
Thousand Oaks (3 times)
Toledo (5 times)
Toronto* (3 times)
Tucson (5 times)
Tulsa (3 times)
Vancouver* (4 times)
Wallingford
Washington (6 times)
Waterbury
West Palm Beach (3 times)
West Point (twice)
Wichita (twice)
Wilmington (twice)
Winnipeg* (3 times)
Worcester

US TOUR 5
Appleton
Baltimore
Calgary*
Charlotte
Chicago
Dallas
Denver
Des Moines
Durham
Edmonton*
Grand Rapids
Greenville
Hartford
Indianapolis
Kansas City
Little Rock
Louisville
Madison
McAllen
Milwaukee
Nashville
Norfolk
Ottawa
Philadelphia
Portland
Providence
San Diego
San Francisco
Schenectady
Seattle
Tempe
Vancouver*
Washington

*Canadian visit

ROTTERDAM

SINGAPORE

DUBLIN

PARIS

SHANGHAI

BERLIN

SAN SEBASTIAN

MELBOURNE

PERTH

CANADA
Toronto, Royal Alexandra Theatre
07.03.89 - 26.05.90
(2 subsequent visits to Toronto)
Ottawa, National Arts Centre
30.07.92 - 15.08.92
Canada Tour 1
09.06.90 – 14.09.91
Canada Tour 2
18.06.92 - 06.02.93

CARIBBEAN
Dominican Republic
Santo Domingo

BERMUDA
Hamilton

CENTRAL & SOUTH AMERICA

ARGENTINA
Buenos Aires

BRAZIL
Sao Paulo (twice)

MEXICO
Mexico City (twice)

EUROPE

AUSTRIA
Vienna
Graz
Innsbruck
Linz
Klagenfurt (twice)
Mastodonterne (twice)
Staatz (twice)
Steyr

BELGIUM
Antwerp

CZECH REPUBLIC
Prague (3 times)
Brno

DENMARK
Copenhagen (3 times)
Aalborg (twice)
Aarhus (3 times)
Herning (3 times)
Holstebro
Juelsminde
Maribo
Odense
Silkeborg
Varde
Vejle

ESTONIA
Tallinn (3 times)
Tartu

FINLAND
Helsinki
Tampere
Turku

FRANCE
Paris, Palais des Sports
Originating production
17.09.80 - 14.12.80
2 subsequent visits

GERMANY
Berlin
Bad Hersfeld
Baden (twice)
Bonn
Chemnitz
Dessau (twice)
Detmold
Duisburg
Fuessen
Gera
Heidelberg
Hof
Lubeck
Luneburg
Magdeburg
Meiningen
Pforzheim
Regensburg
Saarbrucken
Tecklenburg (twice)
Xanten

HOLLAND
Amsterdam (twice)
Rotterdam
Scheveningen

HUNGARY
Budapest (3 times)
Györ
Kecskemet
Miskolc
Szeged
Székésfehérvár

ICELAND
Reykjavik (3 times)

LUXEMBOURG
Wiltz

NORWAY
Oslo (3 times)
Bergen
Bolmo
Kristiansand
Lillestrom
Sandnes
Tromso
Trondheim

POLAND
Gydnia
Lodz
Warsaw

SERBIA
Belgrade

SLOVAKIA
Bratislava

SLOVENIA
Maribor

SPAIN
Madrid (twice)
Alicante
Barcelona (twice)
Bilbao
Burgos
Coruña
Gijon
Granada
Las Palmas
Logrono
Malaga
Mallorca
Murcia
Pamplona
Salamanca
San Sebastian
Santander
Seville (twice)
Tenerife
Valencia (twice)
Valladolid
Vigo
Zaragoza

SWEDEN
Stockholm
Gothenburg
Jönköping
Karlstad (twice)
Malmo (twice)

SWITZERLAND
Lausanne
St Gallen
Thun

MIDDLE EAST
Israel
Tel Aviv (4 times)
Jerusalem
Haifa

UNITED ARAB EMIRATES
Dubai

SOUTH AFRICA
Cape Town

INDIAN OCEAN
Mauritius
Mahebourg

FAR EAST

CHINA
Shanghai

HONG KONG

KOREA
Seoul (4 times)
Busan
Daegu (twice)
Yongin

JAPAN
Tokyo (18 times)
11.06.87 - 30.11.87
Celebrated 30th anniversary of its original Tokyo opening in June 2017
Nagoya (8 times)
Osaka (8 times)
Sendai (twice)
Sapporo
Fukuoka (4 times)
Kanazawa
Matsumoto
Toyama
Shizuoka City
Aichi

PHILIPPINES
Manila (twice)

SINGAPORE (3 times)

AUSTRALIA AND NEW ZEALAND

Sydney, Theatre Royal
20.11.87 - 15.07.89

Melbourne, Princess Theatre
07.12.89 - 29.09.90

Perth, His Majesty's Theatre
11.10.90 - 22.11.90

Adelaide, Festival Theatre
01.01.91 - 03.03.91

Brisbane, Lyric Theatre
08.03.91 - 18.05.91

Auckland, Aotea Centre
28.05.91 - 17.08.91

10TH ANNIVERSARY TOUR
Sydney
Melbourne
Auckland
Perth
Brisbane

25TH ANNIVERSARY TOUR
Melbourne
Perth
Sydney
Brisbane

All dates correct to 9/10/2018

CHAPTER 11

The School Edition

Late on a Friday in May 2001 Cameron Mackintosh was driven through the rush-hour traffic from New York City to Holy Trinity High School in upstate Hicksville. There, an important test was taking place. Could *Les Mis* be adapted successfully for performances in schools – and would schoolchildren be able to cope with the challenges posed by top music professionals?

Above, left to right: The programme for the Welsh language premiere of the *Les Misérables* School Edition, Millennium Centre, Cardiff, 2005; A promotional leaflet advertising the *Les Misérables* School Edition, 2003; The programme for *Les Misérables* School Edition, All Saints, Hove, 2006; Programme for Dauntsey's School, Devizes' concert performance, Prince of Wales Theatre, London, 2003.

Freddie Gershon, chairman of Music Theatre International (MTI), which licenses shows for professional and amateur companies all over the world, remembered Cameron getting increasingly excited as the show proceeded. The impresario was won over by a production that, said Gershon, "went like a dream – and ended with Cameron giving careful notes about absolutely everything all the way back to New York".

Two more test runs – one at a high school in Levittown, Pennsylvania, the other a performance by teenagers in a theatre in Nyack, New York – clinched it. The *Les Misérables* School Edition, a version reduced to some two hours' running time and adapted for young voices, was a goer. And what a goer it has proved! In America alone, MTI has licensed over 3,000 productions, watched by an estimated seven million people since the scheme began. There have been others in countries ranging from Egypt to Nepal, France to Uruguay.

Mackintosh himself had long been keen on such a project. *Les Mis* is, he said, "ideal material for students, since it's got so many wonderful parts and it's about aspiration, about survival, about the triumph of the spirit, about everything you need to grow up in this wicked world". Moreover, it would obviously help to interest a new generation in the theatre.

Indeed, *Les Mis* has already revealed that there is abundant talent in the age range the school edition permits, which is 19 or under. At the end of the closing performance of the first Broadway production in 2003 the cast stepped aside, giving way to a crowd of ragged figures singing "At the End of the Day". "They pulled off their rags, and the audience realized they were 16, 17, 18 years old," remembered Gershon. "Then a young boy or girl would sing in a voice that wasn't trained but had this wonderful innocence and purity. It was impossible to be a living human being and not be shedding tears."

It was much the same when *Les Mis* celebrated its 20th anniversary in London. Schools and young people's groups had been invited to send in videos of particularly successful performers, from which 35 were selected. The chosen teenagers ended up on the stage of the Queen's Theatre, some singing individual numbers and all taking part in the ensemble. Several now have professional careers: Rhidian Marc, James Gant and Alistair Brammer to name but three.

Brammer was stunning proof of the scheme's worth. Here was the son of an Exmouth gardener, the youngest of seven children; he had never been to the theatre or even visited London as a boy, yet was playing Marius as a professional in the West End just five years after that propitious moment in 2005. It was only when he was onstage at the Queen's, looking down at an auditorium he found impossibly grand, that he thought, yes, he would like to make this his job.

Brammer eventually spent 18 months as Marius in the West End, as well as taking the role of the student Prouvaire in the film of *Les Mis*. "I should be sick to death of the show," he said, "but I can't get over it. It's my favourite."

Most importantly of all the first production of the School Edition at Penarth in Wales was to prove the catalyst for the new life of *Les Misérables*.

Left: Musical Youth Company, Oxford, 2004.

Clockwise from top left: Beaconhurst School, Stirling, 2009; React Theatre Productions, Hove, 2006; Stretch Youth Theatre Company, Dartford, 2008; US school production at the Civic Amarillo, 2003: Minerva Youth Theatre, Glasgow, 2010; US school production at North Central High School, Spokane, 2004; Musical Youth Company, Oxford, 2004; Horncastle Upstagers, Horncastle, 2010; (centre) Stoke Youth Musical Theatre Company, Stoke-on-Trent, 2008.

One Decade More!

This picture: Thirty-five of the most talented children from school productions joined the cast at the Queen's Theatre, London, to celebrate the 20th anniversary, 8 October 2005.

Devon schoolboy Alistair Brammer as Marius, Centre Stage, Exmouth, 2005, who went on to play the same role in the West End in 2009 and the part of Jean Prouvaire in the film.

CHAPTER 12

Moving Down Shaftesbury Avenue

'Red and Black' makes way for *The Woman in White.*

Some productions take their show on the road, as *Les Misérables* has done on a global scale. But in 2004, the production travelled closer to home – moving after more than 18 years and over 7500 performances quite literally down the street from one Shaftesbury Avenue address (the Palace, its home since December 1985) to another (the Queen's, where it is playing to this day). And with barely a week between closing at the larger Palace on 27 March 2004, and resuming at the smaller and, by that point, more suitable Queen's on 3 April. The company – headed by Jeff Leyton as Jean Valjean, Michael McCarthy as Javert, and S Club pop star Jon Lee as Marius – remained intact.

Shifting venues within the same city is not unusual: *Mamma Mia!* has played three West End houses, and Stephen Daldry's production of *An Inspector Calls* has bounced all over town. But when Andrew Lloyd Webber made clear a desire to reclaim his 1450-seat Cambridge Circus venue for the premiere of his musical *The Woman in White*, Mackintosh seized the opportunity to consider the surroundings of *Les Misérables* afresh. Using a reconfigured design and smaller orchestra would allow a new lease of life for the production at the 1100-seat Queen's at a time when business at the Palace was beginning to slow.

The success of the Schools' version had proven the elasticity of the material and suggested to Mackintosh that the original London production could withstand a new home even if, the producer recalls, "it wasn't game, set and match" – nothing in this business is ever a sure bet.

It helped, of course, that Mackintosh had recently bought the freehold of the adjacent Queen's and Gielgud Theatres, so could act as his own landlord, and that the remaining two-year lease on the Queen's still held by Lloyd Webber's Really Useful Theatres would revert to Mackintosh immediately.

But was he not nervous about the move? "For the audience, there were a lot of pluses about the Queen's," says Mackintosh, keen at the same time to acknowledge the "grandeur" conferred upon the show at the Palace, which in its design really is a small-scale opera house. Given that nearly 400 out of the Palace's ample seating capacity are in the balcony, the intimacy of the Queen's meant that more people could enjoy the show from the increased number of better seats and sightlines. "It was a real gamble," says Mackintosh, recalling a gradual build in profits at the Queen's until, within the fourth year, the show was "back to capacity – something it hadn't

Right: Longest Running Show plaque inset into the pavement outside Queen's Theatre, London

Below: Invitation card to a drinks party to bid farewell to *Les Misérables* featuring Cosette moving down to Queen's Theatre on a Routemaster bus, March 2004; Cameron Mackintosh and Andrew Lloyd Webber outside the Palace Theatre, London when *Les Mis* was about to move, March 2004.

DREAM THE DREAM
Les Misérables
THE WORLD'S LONGEST RUNNING MUSICAL
QUEENS THEATRE
Les Misérabl
Les Misérables
DREAM THE DREAM
THE WORLD'S LONGEST RUNNING MUSICAL
'STILL LIKE A FIRST NIGHT'
QUEEN'S THEATRE
A musical by
ALAIN BOUBLIL & CLAUDE-MICHEL SCHÖNBERG
THE WORLD'S LONGEST RUNNING MUSICAL
'STILL LIKE A FIRST NIGHT'

A TRULY MOVING
EXPERIENCE!
Les Misérables
ARRIVES AT
THE QUEEN'S THEATRE APRIL 2004
www.lesmis.com

been for well over a decade at the Palace". (One buoyant by product of the move was that it allowed Judi Dench, who was appearing next door at the Gielgud in Shakespeare's *All's Well That Ends Well*, to dash down the street during a 45-minute break and join the barricade scene for one performance on 6 May 2004: a starry cameo if there ever was one.)

Bedded into its cosier and enduring home, the show was then poised on 7 October 2006, to enter record books as the longest-running musical in West End history.

With the benefit of hindsight, Mackintosh can speak of the move "being exactly the right thing to happen at that point in its life, just as the Palace was the perfect place for the musical to become this legend."

"What I didn't realise," the producer adds, "is what we had unleashed." There was considerably more excitement still to come.

Above: Promotional card featuring youthful cast members Oliver Thornton, Sophia Ragavelas and, member of former pop group S Club 7, Jon Lee, at the time *Les Misérables* moved London theatres.

Right: Backstage at Queen's Theatre, 2015.

CHAPTER 13

Let the People Sing

Altogether, *Les Misérables* has had a rich life outside the professional theatre and, indeed, outside theatres themselves. It has become famous for big planned events, but on 11 April 2009 the musical received an even bigger boost from a single person – one that nobody had planned.

The impact of *Les Misérables* is felt well beyond the countless auditoriums where the show has been performed. Over time, the musical has entered the zeitgeist in ways few could have anticipated, not least on that night over Easter weekend, 2009, when an ordinary-seeming woman whom no one had ever heard of had an extraordinary and catalytic effect upon the fate of *Les Misérables* going forward.

That person, of course, was Susan Boyle, an unemployed Scot who had seen the production on tour in Edinburgh and whose rendition of "I Dreamed a Dream" on the third series of *Britain's Got Talent* became an immediate sensation and went through the stratosphere on YouTube. To this day, the initial scepticism of the TV panel remains online for all to see, giving way to euphoria – make that adulation – as the miner's daughter from Blackburn, West Lothian, visibly commits to the song from someplace deep within.

"She sang very, very well," Claude-Michel Schönberg remarked admiringly of Boyle, "but in her case I thought the lyrics were more important than the music. She was saying, 'I wish I had another life,' and I was flabbergasted because it was so poignant and true."

Mackintosh recalls heading to the country that Friday and glimpsing a newspaper item about "I Dreamed a Dream" being performed as part of that week's competitive line up on Simon Cowell's popular reality TV franchise. "So Michael

Above: Cameron Mackintosh shaking hands with Bill Clinton, Kennedy Center, Washington, 11 June 1994.

Right: Susan Boyle sings "I Dreamed a Dream" during the *Britain's Got Talent* live tour in 2009. Boyle shot to fame after performing Fantine's signature song on the show, and has since become a bestselling performer.

Right, insert: Cover for Susan Boyle's debut album, "I Dreamed A Dream" released in 2009.

Top: *Les Misérables* flash mob at St Pancras station, London, 13 May 2013, at which 1,000 people gathered and sang "Do You Hear The People Sing" to celebrate the release of the film on DVD.

Middle, left: Caricature by Morten Morland of the then Chancellor Alastair Darling on budget day singing "I Dreamed A Dream" which had just become a global phenomenon following Susan Boyle's performance on the TV show *Britain's Got Talent*. Published in *The Times*, 20 April 2009.

Middle: Hillary Clinton used the phrase "a basket of deplorables" in her presidential campaign which Donald Trump and his team adopted. Trump is seen here in front of their adapted banner at a rally in Miami, September 2016.

Middle, right: Cartoon by Nicholas Garland depicting David Cameron as Cosette outside London's Palace Theatre when he was negotiating with the EU over budget increases. *Daily Telegraph*, 29 October 2010.

[Mackintosh's partner] and I sat down to watch it, knowing absolutely nothing" – and the rest, as they say, is history.

The result? "Every news reader around the world started talking about 'I Dreamed a Dream' from *Les Misérables*, and, although there were already more than 40 cast albums in existence, for the very first time in 25 years, *Les Mis* had a hit song." Before Boyle, notes Mackintosh, "the songs had become standards but never hits": the stand-alone power of the music carved an unforeseen place in the public consciousness, which in turn reaped numerous benefits, not least gathering interest in the pending movie. It's perhaps no accident that Anne Hathaway won an Oscar for singing the very same song in the film.

Even as Boyle went on to navigate a newfound career that included a film of her own life, *Les Misérables* found its score reaching out to people in all circumstances the world over whether they be in prison, in military barracks or of contrasting political stripes. The day before the 2008 presidential election, Barack Obama's campaign staff posted their version of "One Day More" – Les Misbarack – on YouTube, to this day a masterpiece of expert lip-syncing.

Above: The student Occupy Central pro-democracy demonstration in Hong Kong where they sang adapted lyrics of "Do You Hear the People Sing?" as their protest anthem, September 2014.

Above, insert: Cover for the deluxe CD of the film soundtrack, 2013.

Right: Alumni of the West End casts of *Les Misérables* sing "Do You Hear the People Sing?", the favourite musical song of MP Jo Cox at a celebration of her life, Trafalgar Square, London, 22 June 2016.

Below, right: CDs (clockwise from top right) Czech cast recording, 2011; French cast recording, 1991; Korean cast recording, 1993; Highlights from the Complete Symphonic International cast recording, 1992; Antwerp cast recording, 1998 and the Netherlands cast album, 2008.

And while Bill Clinton used "One Day More" as a campaign song in 1992, his wife Hillary several decades later used the phrase "a basket of deplorables" in her own presidential campaign. That, in turn, prompted Donald Trump's opposing team to respond with a digital banner bearing the words "Les Deplorables," and co-opting "Do You Hear the People Sing?" for a Trump rally in Miami in September 2016. "These songs have become a part of the popular culture," says Mackintosh of an unstoppable increase in the reach of the score that has surfaced in flash mobs at railway stations and weddings, student demonstrations as far afield as Turkey and Hong Kong, and has been adopted by caricaturists aplenty such as Al Hirschfeld and Nicholas Garland. A special limited-run, student-led production of the show, put together by the community, was held in August 2017 in the Yorkshire constituency of the murdered MP Jo Cox, whose favourite musical was *Les Misérables*.

Numerologists, incidentally, might want to note the value of five-digit numbers in relation to a show whose central character has prison number 24601 whereas Susan Boyle's contestant number was 43212. In a show whose numbers are off the charts, these two are surely worth remembering.

Clockwise from top: Programme for performances at Erlestoke Prison, Wiltshire, March 2012; Programme for *Les Misérables*, presented by Pimlico Opera, in the form of an adapted Monopoly board, Wandsworth Prison, London, March 2007; Booking leaflet, illustrated with the Bishop of Digne's silver candlesticks, for the performances at Wandsworth Prison, March 2007; The Pimlico Opera production at High Down Prison, Surrey, October 2017.

CHAPTER 14

Les Misérables In Concert

Royal endorsement of the West End musical and its presentation on an epic scale.

Les Misérables thinks big and delivers big, at no place more so than in concert. The first concert staging of the musical in Sydney on Australia Day in January 1989, drew what remains its largest-ever single audience of more than 125,000 people. At the vast Skydome in Toronto, a *Les Misérables* concert in August 1989, played to more people than had The Rolling Stones. Concert tours have been cross-country sensations in Scandinavia and Japan.

When the Queen was celebrating 100 years of the Anglo-French Entente Cordiale with President Jacques Chirac and Prime Minister Tony Blair, it was *Les Misérables* she invited to entertain her guests at Windsor Castle in November 2004. Waving tricolours and Union flags embossed with the Cosette logo, Mackintosh and a jubilant cast left an early-evening performance at the Queen's Theatre. Heading for Windsor in a police motorcade, they gave an abridged performance in which Michael Ball stepped up to the role of Valjean, following a State Banquet in the Waterloo Chamber. At the end, the royal party and their guests did not want to leave a show that left President Chirac declaring that he understood why it had run for 20 years – "and now I want to come back and see the whole thing".

A 10th anniversary concert at London's Royal Albert Hall ended with 17 international Valjeans coming onstage, each accompanied by a Gavroche holding his national flag. Three concert performances in the Hollywood Bowl in 2008 featured American actor and musical theatre star Brian Stokes Mitchell as Javert and Lea Michele, leading lady in the musical-comedy series *Glee* (who played Little Cosette on Broadway in 1996), as Eponine.

But the two performances at London's vast O2 arena on 3 October 2010 were surely the most spectacular so far. Even by Cameron Mackintosh's standards, this was quite the event, amalgamating a starry company of over 500 with a huge choir and a full orchestra, not to mention the 200 teenagers from the school edition who entered through the audience at the end. The occasion played to audiences totalling 33,000 and was beamed to over 1,000 cinemas in Britain, Europe, America, Australia and the Far East. The American TV channel PBS screened the concert regularly for two years, reigniting Hollywood interest that led directly to the film.

This time, Valjean was played by opera singer Alfie Boe, Javert by Broadway's Norm Lewis, Thénardier by Matt Lucas and Marius by a young singer with a huge following in America: Nick Jonas from the Jonas Brothers. He had been playing Gavroche when the show closed on Broadway in 2003 and had so impressed Mackintosh that he asked him to come back and audition for Marius when he grew up. They and the other performers entered in full costume, only to be added to for the finale by numerous show alumni, among them Colm Wilkinson, John Owen-Jones, and Simon Bowman joining Boe to deliver Schönberg's new arrangement of his most moving song, "Bring Him Home". There was not a dry eye in that vast arena.

Above: Cameron Mackintosh introduces Her Majesty The Queen to the cast, Windsor Castle, 2004.

Right: DVD cover for the Windsor Castle Concert, 2004.

Top row: Tenth Anniversary Concert, Royal Albert Hall, 1995; souvenir brochure cover.

Middle row: Party invitation for the 25th Anniversary Concert at London's O2, 2010; The Valjean Quartet, Simon Bowman, Alfie Boe, Colm Wilkinson and John Owen-Jones, after singing "Bring Him Home"; Cameron Mackintosh (centre) celebrates with the original Eponine, Frances Ruffelle, and the concert Eponine, Samantha Barks, who was also to become the film Eponine. Concert Cosette, Katie Hall, and the original Cosette, Rebecca Caine, join in the fun.

Bottom row: SkyDome, Toronto, 1989; Australia Day Concert, Sydney, 1989 and advertisement.

Following pages: The finale of the 25th Anniversary Concert, which featured the original London company, the Queen's Theatre company, the UK tour company and the 25th anniversary company, at the O2, London, 3 October 2010.

CHAPTER 15

Les Misérables Re-Born: The 25th Anniversary Production

Cameron Mackintosh had seen many professional stagings of *Les Misérables* around the world from Tel Aviv to Budapest, but it was not until 2002 when he went to see the first British school edition production of what would become thousands worldwide, in the small Welsh town of Penarth, that something more than pleasure at its brilliant, inventive designs, totally conceived by the school, stirred in his mind. Must the staging that had first appeared at the Barbican Theatre in 1985 really be the definitive – or, even, the only – one?

As the show hurtled towards its 25th anniversary, Mackintosh decided to develop a production that would be brand new in three essential ways. There would be new set designs and a totally different staging. However, first off would be new, more timeless, orchestrations able to serve a 19th-century plot yet freshen the musical and excite audiences now used to a greater sophistication of sound than was available to John Cameron when he arranged the score for the Palais des Sports in 1980.

That last goal needed to be realised from the off, so the intention was to try out the new orchestrations in the Broadway revival that opened at New York's Broadhurst Theatre in November 2006, with Alexander Gemignani (himself the son of famous Broadway conductor, Paul Gemignani) as Valjean and Norm Lewis as Javert. Already, the British orchestra, which had numbered 24 at the Palace, had been downsized to fit the smaller pit at the Queen's. But in a production otherwise boasting the original creative team, the score would here be completely re-orchestrated for 14 musicians, all of whom had to be of soloist standard. The challenge was considerable: inspired by John Cameron's orchestrations the American orchestrator Christopher Jahnke was to bring a fresh ear to the musical in collaboration with Claude-Michel Schönberg and Stephen Metcalfe, a *Les Mis* veteran who is Mackintosh's head of music. Their task was to make more out of less: one cellist, for instance, where there might have once have been six, pressed into the service of an edgier, grittier sound.

Under the baton of musical supervisor Stephen Brooker, the new orchestrations had been initially tried out in London to mixed results, and Brooker admitted to apprehension about a much-revised version arriving on Broadway where, he knew, many audience members loved the show as it had been. "We didn't want to go too far, but we knew that if we didn't dip our toes deep into the water we could end up with a limp adaptation. There were phone calls between our hotel rooms, wondering, 'Oh God, have we messed it up?' I had sleepless nights wondering if we'd done the right thing."

Above: Enjolras and the students wave the red flag of revolution in the 25th anniversary production, which opened at the Wales Millennium Centre, Cardiff, 2010.

They had: the American response was strong, as it was again in Holland in 2008. By that point, Mackintosh, Schönberg and the team knew they had the orchestrations they could use for what would be major milestones in *Les Mis*'s forward march: the spectacular celebratory concert at London's O2 arena and a freshly imagined 25th anniversary production that would look at the material anew, while, says Mackintosh, being sure "not to throw

Above: Jon Robyns as Enjolras, John Owen Jones as Jean Valjean and Gareth Gates as Marius in the UK tour, 2010.

the baby out with the bathwater". Brooker spoke of the very first two notes of the show accomplishing the essential in their newfound ability to "knock the audience's heads off with a sort of metallic mallet". The intention was a staging that would do the same.

"If it ain't broke, why fix it?" might be an obvious response to all this activity, and Trevor Nunn was quick to make known in print his displeasure with the notion of a staging that might supersede his and John Caird's original. But Mackintosh held his ground, arguing the same value in reinvention that Nunn had practised first-hand during his years spent re-examining the repertoire first at the Royal Shakespeare Company and then at the National.

The producer had decided after 25 years of that first *Les Mis* "that the best present I could give the show was a new, younger creative team that in any normal circumstances would have happened naturally with any decent show anyway." Keenly aware of "how many people loved the original, and you can't wipe that away," Mackintosh wanted a production that would be "as good [but] in a different way": an approach that could honour what had come before while moving it forward, at which point his new collaborators began to identify themselves.

To direct, he tapped two former ensemble members of the show, James Powell and Laurence Connor, the second of whom had, in fact, been dance captain years back on the UK tour. Having left behind performing to work as a director, Connor demurred at the start: "I thought, 'Why would you do any different version? The first one was so beloved.'" Beyond that, he added, "I hadn't actually worked with anybody before as a co-director, and was concerned with how you do that when it is clearly one person's vision that is called for."

On the other hand, the initial English *Les Mis* had been the directorial vision of two men, Nunn and Caird, and it wasn't long before Connor saw the sense in a dual perspective whereby Powell's understanding of certain key moments in the show – Enjolras, for instance, waving the red flag –

dovetailed with Connor's interest in "looking at the story as a piece of drama and starting to re-evaluate how we tell that story".

One obvious mode of reassessment was visual, and the directors worked closely with a newly appointed design team in Matt Kinley (sets) and Paule Constable (lighting). Christine Rowland also designed a number of new costumes to go alongside many of Andreane Neofitou's original designs which gave an important continuity to the whole. Kinley took as his point of departure an awareness of paintings by Victor Hugo which he thought "beautiful and absolutely right for *Les Misérables*, with great chiaroscuro, wonderful light and dark, brooding and threatening, yet with an amazing romantic feel".

He showed them to Mackintosh, who asked if they were by Turner, which was a good guess given that Hugo was undoubtedly influenced by the great Romantic-era painter. Hugo's art evoked clouds, townscapes and the land in a style that could be called impressionistic or even surreal, embellished or so it appeared with anything that could lighten, blacken or colour them: coffee, coal, toothpaste, blackberry juice, ash from the fire.

The idea was to use some of Hugo's sketches, gouaches and watercolours as scene-setting backdrops, though never in ways that would distract the audience. Kinley tried a few of them out in a design for a wide, shallow proscenium in Atlanta, and that had seemed successful – "I was blown away," says Mackintosh and, more importantly, the audience was also happy to embrace this new look to an iconic musical.

John Napier's original set for *Les Misérables* was one of the masterpieces of 20th century stage design and allowed the story to be told with very little on stage apart from a revolve and two large interlocking sculptures, everything else was imagined in the black box. The revolve was particularly clever, enabling scenes to change quickly and be seen from different perspectives as well as acting as a metaphor for Valjean's never ending journey.

So as Kinley says, "There seemed little point in using a revolve as we would invariably repeat what had been done so masterfully before. Also we wanted to take the show out of the black box and illustrate the scenes with time, place and colour. I thought this would be easy, but it soon dawned on me that trying to describe all these scenes with scenery would make the show even bigger than before. The original show was impregnable in its simplicity and at one point I threw in the towel. The breakthrough came when I looked at employing the paintings of Victor Hugo as a moving projected backdrop for the show, this allowed us to change scenes very simply and lyrically and gave a cinematic sweep which, combined with many small moving trucks and staircases, gave us a tool kit to describe all the scenes."

The goal was to allow the paintings projected on to 3D surfaces to coalesce with the extraordinarily atmospheric and dramatic lighting of Paule Constable. "What was amazing was that Cameron was bold enough to reinvent *Les Mis* and that he encouraged us to do that with him," says Constable, speaking from Glyndebourne Festival Opera in Sussex where she was lighting Handel's *Giulio Cesare*. The Tony and Olivier Award winning British lighting designer found in the opera repertoire a direct equivalent to what Mackintosh was doing with *Les Mis* in "allowing each generation to claim and interpret a piece so that it is not preserved in aspic but is told from a contemporary perspective, just as Trevor and John and David [Hersey, the original lighting designer] did" when they got the job. They in turn had reinvented the show from the very first 1980 Paris production directed by Robert Hossein and his team.

The factory where Fantine worked would, for instance, be seen from the inside rather than impressionistically from the outside, and the women would be polishing jet, as indicated by Hugo. The audience would hear the sound of a factory whistle accompanying orchestrations that Connor felt possessed what might be called a "brutal pulse" in keeping with the greater realism of his team's aesthetic.

Everywhere the aim was to bolster that needed realism. The original actors in the new production that opened in December 2009 at the Wales Millennium Centre in Cardiff were, in Connor's words, "to live their story, rather than seeming to explain that 'this is my plight'". There would be more colour, more sense of location. The clouds would gently move, or factory smoke rise, in projections of Hugo's paintings – what Kinley calls "a moving backcloth". In performance terms, Madalena Alberto's Fantine was not a glamorous leading lady but a broken woman who had been spat at and horribly misused; Ashley Artus's Thénardier, while still raising the odd laugh, was a voracious human weasel; and John Owen-Jones, as Valjean, now emphasized the newly released convict's brutishness, with his matted hair and vagrant looks helping to explain why everyone from innkeepers to factory foremen rejected him.

Opposite: "Lovely Ladies" from the 25th anniversary production.

Left: Matt Kinley's original design for "Stars" for the 25th anniversary production, 2010.

There were other innovations, too. Powell remembers a struggle with the opening, which had always shown convicts labouring in the fields. They asked Mackintosh's PA to send two bottles of wine to Kinley's studio, where they sat in the dark and drank, listening to Schönberg's pulsating score with eyes closed. "I said, 'They're rowing'," recalled Powell. And so the stony field became a galley, an idea endorsed by the composer, who emailed to say "that's very interesting because when I first composed this I imagined exactly that".

Film projections helped, too, in bringing to the fore Parisian sewers that stretched into the distance and a sensational suicide for Earl Carpenter's terrifying Javert. Thanks to technical trickery that the team is loath to explain, he appeared to throw himself through misty air into a seething, swirling Seine. With adaptable "sliders" or panels speedily bringing onstage fresh scenic effects, one saw notably towering Paris slums beneath which the poor scurried like mice: the result was simultaneously intense and spectacular, as required.

Kinley speaks with pride of a production that was "full of colour and light," just as Constable describes "working on a living, breathing painting; the whole thing felt as if it breathed more, and that includes the score."

The original production hadn't toured for over a decade, and Mackintosh remembers fans at the Wales opening telling him it was their favourite show of all time. "I said to them, 'No, this is different,' and they would say, 'Yes, it's a new cast,' and I would say, 'No, it's a new everything.'" And by the interval, "they would see me and say, 'It's still my favourite show but it's never been as good as this before'". A second *Les Mis* had been minted that could more than hold its own alongside the original. "Our only mistake," Mackintosh says of this UK tour "is that we under booked it."

As well as touring the UK the show returned to its English birthplace, the Barbican, for three weeks in autumn 2010. Would the London critics again be mixed about "The Glums"? On the contrary: *The Daily Telegraph* was "stirred and exhilarated" by the music, the story and the evening's "sheer passion and pace," and the *Guardian* found the show "shamelessly entertaining". The two 25th anniversary O2 arena concerts, again with Connor and Powell at the helm, added to a surge of renewed interest that proved the greatest birthday gift any show could have.

Before long the new production was also touring America, Japan, Korea, Australia, Spain, Mexico and Brazil. It captured the imagination of the film company Working Title as well as the director Tom Hooper and executives from Universal, all of whom caught it at various destinations across the Atlantic. *Les Mis* was about to play to its biggest audience ever.

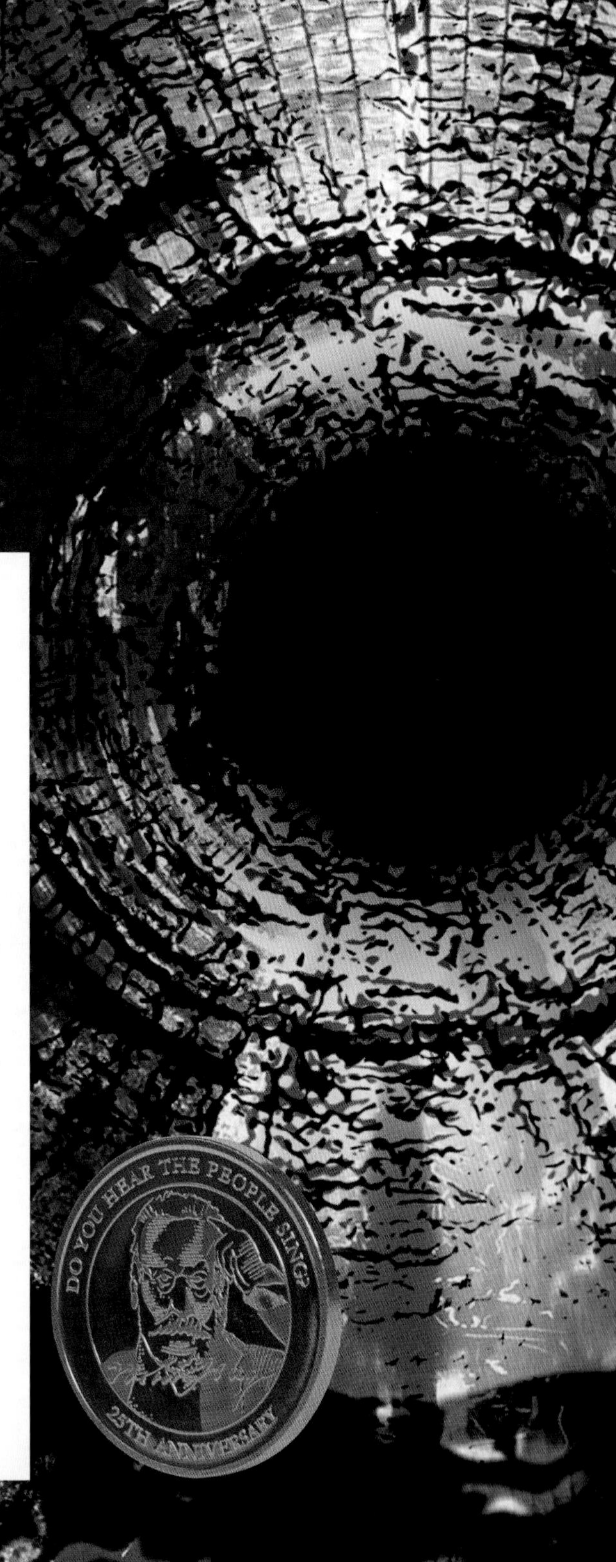

Above, left: The show's sets, such as these Paris slums, have only grown more evocative as the years have progressed.

Left: Joonmo Yang as Valjean sings the Soliloquy, Japan, 2015.

Right: A commemorative coin to celebrate the 25th anniversary.

Opposite: A poster for *Les Misérables'* special return run at London's Barbican Theatre in celebration of the show's 25th anniversary in 2010.

Background: Matt Kinley's original design for the Sewers for the 25th anniversary production, 2010.

THE NEW 25TH ANNIVERSARY PRODUCTION
THE BARBICAN • 22 PERFS ONLY

CHAPTER 16

The Journey to the Screen

There have, of course, been numerous film versions of Victor Hugo's novel dating back a hundred years, but never a cinematic version of the musical.

In 1912, Henry Krauss starred as Jean Valjean for director Albert Capellani's silent version and later played Monseigneur Myriel in Raymond Bernard's 1934 adaptation. Hollywood first took up the challenge in 1935 with Charles Laughton being nominated for an Oscar® as Javert, and then again in 1952 when the Moldovan-born, American director Lewis Milestone – an Oscar® winner for the anti-war epic *All Quiet on the Western Front* – cast Michael Rennie (best known for the original version of *The Day The Earth Stood Still)* as Valjean and fellow Brit Robert Newton (who found fame as Long John Silver in *Treasure Island*) as his nemesis, Javert.

"I added up all the film and television versions of *Les Misérables* that have been done, including *The Fugitive*, which is a modern retelling of the story, and there are over forty," said Cameron Mackintosh. "Every few years someone would say 'I want to do my version of *Les Misérables*', but no one has ever done a musical. Until now."

Hollywood is always on the lookout for a powerful, emotional story that will resonate with a mass audience and in 1987 New York was buzzing as *Les Misérables* played sell-out shows day after day at the Broadway Theatre. With advance ticket sales of $12 million (a phenomenal sum at the time) *Les Misérables* was a guaranteed success and the power players in California duly took note and beat a path to Mackintosh's door.

Columbia Tri-Star, at that time relatively new on the Hollywood scene, had been set up by the studio giant Sony Pictures and was looking for hot projects to establish its credentials. *Les Misérables* fitted the bill perfectly. "It was right at the birth of Tri-Star and they wanted the rights," said Mackintosh, "and I said that, yes, I would be interested depending on who directed it."

Mackintosh wanted Alan Parker, the British director who had directed *Fame* and *Bugsy Malone*, a small-budget, British musical that cast kids as Chicago gangsters.

"Alan was booked to do it," Mackintosh recalled, "and I thought he was a great choice, a great director who understood the music. We even took out ads in the trade papers announcing it."

But although Mackintosh was keen on the film project he was also understandably protective of his stage show. He did not want a film to appear too soon because that, potentially, could have damaged the Broadway and London productions: "I was adamant that we wouldn't make the film immediately because we had just opened the show on Broadway. So I said, 'Look, it can't be released for a few years ...' And they agreed that we would wait and make it five years after the Broadway opening."

On stage *Les Misérables* went from strength to strength and the film was put on a back burner. Alan Parker went off to direct other films, including *Evita* with Madonna as Eva Peron.

"A couple of other directors came on board but it never got there," said Mackintosh, "and thank God it didn't happen then is all I can say. I didn't despair because within a few years I had 15 productions of *Les Misérables* running around the world." This is still today a record for simultaneous productions running at one time.

"I was just thrilled that the (movie) rights came back to me from Tri-Star because it hadn't been made. And at that time musicals on film weren't nearly as popular."

As Mackintosh pointed out, over the years, other musicals have paved the way for *Les Misérables* to be adapted for the screen. "I think we're making this movie now because Baz Luhrmann did *Moulin Rouge*, *Evita* was made, *Chicago* went to the big screen successfully, *Mamma Mia!* was a huge hit. And with all of those the appetite for the film musical has grown."

In 2010, Mackintosh felt that it was the right time to push the film project forward. He approached Working Title, the British-based film production company with a hugely successful track record – *Four Weddings and a Funeral, Dead Man Walking, Elizabeth, Bridget Jones's Diary, Pride and Prejudice, Anna Karenina* and many more – and met with Eric Fellner, Tim Bevan and Debra Hayward, who would all become producers on the film. Working Title has a long and fruitful partnership with Universal, the American studio, who would green light the project.

"Cameron brought *Les Misérables* to Working Title in early 2010 and we started looking for a writer to adapt it for the screen. We all agreed that Bill Nicholson would be perfect for the screenplay," said Hayward.

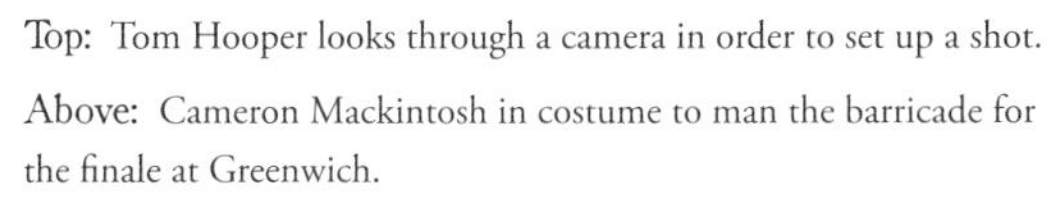

Top: Tom Hooper looks through a camera in order to set up a shot.

Above: Cameron Mackintosh in costume to man the barricade for the finale at Greenwich.

Right: Film producers Cameron Mackintosh and Debra Hayward chat with Ben Howarth on a snowy street set.

Above, left: Tom Hooper setting up a scene with Dan Channing-Williams.

Above, right: Eric Fellner, one of the film producers, enjoys a joke on set.

Right: Aaron Tveit as Enjolras and Eddie Redmayne as Marius brandish their weapons while Hugh Skinner as Joly and Alistair Brammer as Prouvaire hold the flags of revolution.

Overleaf: Actors portraying the poverty-stricken and hungry peasants during the song "Look Down".

Nicholson, who has twice been nominated for an Oscar® (for *Gladiator* and *Shadowlands*), was also crucial in bringing director Tom Hooper on board. The writer mentioned that he was also working on *Les Misérables* and Hooper was immediately intrigued. He took himself off to see the London stage show and, through his contacts at Working Title, let it be known that he was very, very interested in directing the movie.

Independently, Eric Fellner was thinking along the same lines, as he recalled: "We got a screenplay from Bill and I had just seen *The King's Speech*. It was at that first screening in 2010, I think, and I remember going to that early screening and seeing Tom and thinking, 'Wow, wouldn't it be great if we could find something for him …' and it turned out that Tom and Bill were actually friends and Bill had mentioned it to Tom and we thought, 'Well, this would be the perfect choice.'"

Although *The King's Speech* had not yet been generally released, there was a considerable buzz building on both sides of the Atlantic. Mackintosh met Hooper and the two men clearly hit it off. "That was before *The King's Speech* came out, but one of the things that impressed me about Tom was that he took it on himself to go and see the show and I heard from Debra and Eric: 'Tom is very interested.'" said Mackintosh.

"I'd seen *The Damned United* (Hooper's earlier movie about the British football manager Brian Clough) and liked that and then I saw *The King's Speech* and liked that very much too. But when *The King's Speech* became such a huge success, I sat back and thought, 'It may well have been the film he wanted to make before but who knows if he will still want to when he has won an Oscar®?'"

The King's Speech did indeed do well at the Oscars® and Hooper was now a highly sought after filmmaker. The question was: would he still want to direct *Les Misérables* when he was receiving offers from all over Hollywood?

"There was never any doubt," said Hooper. "I knew that this was the film I wanted to make and I didn't waver from that. There were a lot of offers, but *Les Misérables* was the one."

Hooper was already planning how he would take *Les Misérables* from the stage and make it cinematic; the Londoner was passionate about the idea that his actors would perform each and every song live before the cameras – and that convinced Mackintosh that he was indeed the perfect director for the project.

"Tom had immediately grasped where the emotional power of the story lay," said Mackintosh. "At the very core of this story it's about the survival of the human spirit and the music drives that story. It's probably the most successful adaptation of any book in the history of music. Tom was excited about how he would film those great ensemble numbers and record all the performances live. He said to me, 'You know, I would really like to do this live,' which is what I'd dreamed of doing. I knew then that we had found the right man."

Timing, he says, is everything. And a strong belief in fate helps too. "Who knows if *Les Misérables* had opened in any other time than the mid 1980s whether it would have caught the public imagination in the way it did?" noted Mackintosh. "I really believe that it is a blessing that the film wasn't made back when we first started discussing it."

VENTE
LINGE

CHAPTER 17

Close Up on the Director's Vision

Tom Hooper's work, as he has acknowledged, had been grounded in "gritty realism" with hard hitting, illuminating studies of powerful men.

Whether it be a president, a king, a controversial campaigner or an enigmatic, hard drinking football manager, though, there has not been so much as a single song between them.

Hooper cut his creative teeth on television, directing several episodes of the BBC's long-running, prime-time soap, *EastEnders*, before moving on to mini-series. He gained critical attention with the brilliant, BAFTA-winning TV film *Longford* and followed that with the award-winning HBO drama series *John Adams*, chronicling the life of America's second president (played by Paul Giamatti). The show, which won 13 Emmy® Awards, became Hooper's impressive calling card in Hollywood. But instead of heading back to America for his next project, Hooper returned home to make a very British story, directing *The Damned United*.

A year later, Hooper was hard at work on another small budget British production – *The King's Speech*. The film would change his life. With Colin Firth delivering a career-defining performance as King George VI and Geoffrey Rush as Lionel Logue, the unconventional Australian who treats the King's crippling stammer, the film dominated the Oscars® with 12 nominations, winning Best Picture, Best Actor for Firth, Best Director for Hooper and Best Original Screenplay.

After *The King's Speech*, Hooper received a number of offers from major studios for several different genres of film. He surprised everybody – but not himself – by choosing *Les Misérables*. Directing a film based on a musical was a big departure. Or so it seemed.

"Well, weirdly, I could say that I owe being a film director to the musical because when I was eleven or twelve at school, the one thing we did once a year was put on a musical and I was in the school musical for two years running," said Hooper. "I remember I was in the chorus for *The Beggar's Opera* and I had a minor part in Gilbert and Sullivan's *Patience*," he said. "And it allowed two great things to happen: one was to discover that I shouldn't be an actor and the other thing was to discover that I loved directing. It was through those musicals that I discovered a love of drama and theatre and that extended to films."

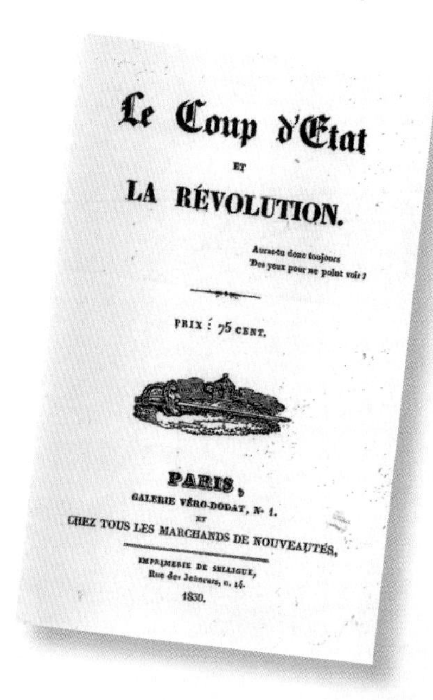
Le Coup d'Etat
ET
LA RÉVOLUTION.

Auras-tu donc toujours
Des yeux pour ne point voir?

PRIX : 75 CENT.

PARIS,
GALERIE VÉRO-DODAT, N° 1.
ET
CHEZ TOUS LES MARCHANDS DE NOUVEAUTÉS,

IMPRIMERIE DE SELLIGUE,
Rue des Jeûneurs, n. 14.
1830.

Left: One of the revolutionary tracts distributed by Marius and the students. These props were based on period documents.

Opposite, above: Members of the cast take a break, while Tom Hooper checks out a few technicalities.

Opposite, below: One of the rebels keeps still as the lighting levels are checked.

In 2010, before *The King's Speech* had been released, Hooper was working on a project with writer William Nicholson, and Nicholson mentioned *Les Misérables* to Hooper.

"When Bill mentioned this to me, I was immediately intrigued and a bell went off in my head," said Hooper. "When I directed *John Adams* for HBO, which is about the American Revolution, I became very interested in the French Revolution as seen from that angle because I hadn't realized that the two revolutions had such an explosive relationship. And, in some ways, the American Revolution is the father of the French Revolution. So the interest in revolutions in France was strongly there.

"So I was attracted to *Les Misérables* and I went to see it and that bell went off even louder. There are moments in the musical when you just get chills down your spine, which to me is a sure sign that there is something special about it."

After meeting the young director, Mackintosh was convinced he had his

VASTES
Draperies et
EXPOSITION
ENTRÉE

man. "A successful project is always about the marriage of many elements that come together at the right time," said Mackintosh. "And we are blessed having a director like Tom who wanted to do this film at this time. We needed a director who embraced the musical form rather than someone who thought the musical form was a nuisance to them in making a film."

Debra Hayward pointed out that Hooper wanted to honour the musical and those who love it and bring in a new audience.

"Part of Tom's vision with the film is that he wants to break down that barrier for people who don't necessarily like musicals. What he's done with the film is to create a world that is really believable – it's immediate; it's real. That time in French history when our story is set was dire and there was a lot of poverty, a lot of grime and dirt and people had to do what they could to survive. Tom shows all of that. It's no holds barred."

For Hooper, that realistic approach to the story meant going back to Victor Hugo's novel and finding the emotional core, drawing on the text to flesh out characters and create a clearer narrative needed for a film. "If there was something I was very proud of with *The King's Speech* it was the emotions it provoked in people. It moved people and that was very satisfying for me.

Opposite: Tom Hooper directs crew at the dry dock at Portsmouth in Hampshire, which has been in existence for over 400 years.

Above: The sheer scale of the scene filmed at Portsmouth, which involved huge water dump tanks and wind machines.

Below: Hugh Jackman and other actors in the chain gang put their all into pulling on the thick, slippery ropes.

"I think the main reason that *Les Misérables* has survived for twenty-seven years is because it mainlines emotion into your body and people go back to it repeatedly because it offers the opportunity to re-experience that emotion with extraordinary consistency and predictability.

"I wanted to do a piece of work that was very much about the heart, from the heart and very emotional. After *The King's Speech*, I loved the idea of doing something utterly different and seizing the opportunity that platform has given me of taking a risk and being ambitious and trying a new genre.

"I have grown up very much in the mode of gritty cinematic realism and I thought what was interesting about this was that, yes, my approach to it is realistic but because it's sung, it's an opportunity to be a little more expressionistic and operatic with my choices and to allow moments sometimes that are heightened reality."

Hooper insisted that the musical's writers, composer Claude-Michel Schönberg and lyricist Alain Boublil, be closely involved with the film. He admired Nicholson's cinematic screenplay, but he also wanted the original writers' instinctive feel for their own material.

"You can't make a film that's just a series of images from the show," said Boublil. "Tom had to make a completely different entity. And I must say our discussions with Tom were wonderfully helpful for us, not least because it helped us learn more about the medium of film. Then we collaborated with Bill Nicholson and we ended up writing together."

Tom made the key early decision to keep dialogue to a minimum and honour the musical's sung-through form: "I wanted to create an alternate reality where people communicate through song rather than having constant gear changes between dialogue and singing."

"At one point we considered having a bigger proportion of dialogue," said Mackintosh. "But Tom felt that the way to do it was to take the show's structure and then dissemble the show and reassemble it for the film. It was like going on a whole new adventure."

Talent from the two different worlds – musical theatre and film – were converging into one, which was vital as Eric Fellner explained, "I thought it was critical that *Les Mis* worked on two levels – it had to work where it still delivered for the fans because the fans are the bedrock of the piece, but it also had to work as a movie in its own right." At first, the collaboration seemed strange, as Debra Hayward commented, "We felt like guests on this project in a way. Because it's such a mature, amazing piece of work and it has this great, long journey before we got involved. And I think you have to understand that to love it.

"Everybody on the film was on a learning curve – the film people who hadn't done a musical before, the musical theatre people who hadn't done a film, actors who hadn't sung on film before, singers who hadn't acted in a film. It's been a great interweaving of all those talents."

There were times, said Schönberg, when he was reminded that movies operate in a very different way than the theatre. "You know they have a luxury that we don't have in the theatre and that came home to me during the auditions. I was looking at an actor and thinking, 'Oh he would be a good guy on the chain gang and then we could use him in the factory and then maybe he could be one of the students, too,' because that's what happens in the theatre – you have someone in one of the lesser roles who can do two or three parts. But obviously it's not like that in movies. They have the luxury of casting an actor for each and every part. I think we had hundreds for *Les Misérables* the film."

In fact, it was over 200 led by a team of Hollywood heavyweights and for each of them, it was to be a challenge quite unlike any other they had faced before.

Above: Set design by Eve Stewart for the film of *Les Misérables*.

Opposite: Hugh Jackman as Jean Valjean peers down the recreated back streets of Paris.

Above: A set plan featuring images of the run-down buildings along the Rue de la Chanvrerie in Paris that were built on T Stage at Pinewood Studios near London.

A5, 6 & 7 DWRG NO. 38

A4 DWRG NO. 37

A1 & 2 DWRG NO. 36

CAFE

DWRG NO

0 NO. 3

B11 DWRG NO. 54

B12 & 13 DWRG NO. 55

B14 DWRG NO. 56

Les Misérables

Rue de la Chanvrerie Elevation - T Stage Scale 1/4" -1'0"

CHAPTER 18

The Dream Cast

Several years ago, Cameron Mackintosh mused over which actors would be perfect for the roles of Jean Valjean and Inspector Javert for the big screen adaptation of *Les Misérables.*

"If you wind the clock back all of those years, I used to think that Hugh Jackman would be Javert and Russell Crowe would be wonderful as Valjean," said Mackintosh.

His casting instincts were spot on even if the roles were, eventually, to be reversed. Hooper and casting director Nina Gold believed that Hugh Jackman was the perfect Valjean, Crowe the ideal Javert. Both actors had strong connections with Mackintosh. Jackman recalled: "Trevor Nunn brought me over to the UK to do *Oklahoma!* in 1998 and that's when I first met Cameron. And for years he'd been asking me to do the stage role of Javert and I wanted to do it but we could never get the timing right."

Crowe, born in New Zealand and raised mostly in Australia, had almost met Mackintosh in Sydney when he was starting out as an actor. "Russell was a friend of a wonderful guy who ran my office there," recalled Mackintosh. "I knew Russell did musicals as I had seen him in *The Blues Brothers*, and he had also done *The Rocky Horror Show* and *Blood Brothers*, before his film career took off. What I didn't know, until he told me, was that he'd auditioned for me for *Miss Saigon*. I said, 'I don't remember seeing you …' And he said, 'No, I wasn't good enough to get to you back then …'"

Crowe's friend was Matthew Dalco, a mate since they were at primary school together. Crowe explained: "Matthew was one of those kids I was very close with. He worked for Cameron in Australia and eventually, in London, and he was one of those guys who believed in me."

Tragically, Matthew, aged just 46, died from cancer in 2009. "It was very, very sad," said Crowe. "He was a lovely guy. When I met Cameron in 2011 and we started having conversations about the possibility of *Les Misérables*, we talked about Matthew a lot. He would definitely have loved this."

Jackman had heard that there was to be a film adaptation of *Les Misérables* via his agent ("a mad *Les Mis* fan") and immediately threw his hat into the ring. For both director Tom Hooper and Mackintosh, he was a natural choice with an impressive record in musical theatre and a beautiful voice that has graced the West End and Broadway.

Jackman was perfect for *Les Misérables*. But the question remained, for which role? "I'd always been asked to play Javert, but I started thinking, 'You know what? I think I'm more Valjean.' But I needed to convince Tom and Cameron. Then they told me that they were thinking the same way and that Russell was in the frame for Javert. And I could totally see that. For me, Valjean just felt better. I just felt more empathy and closer to that character and so I auditioned for Valjean."

Jackman arrived for the audition in New York well prepared. "I'd seen the musical three times, I'd listened to the CD a hundred times. I knew those songs. So I went in and there was Stephen Brooker, the musical director, a pianist, Nina Gold, the casting director and Tom. And I could see Tom thinking, 'Can this guy do it?' And we went through the songs again and again. It went on for about four hours and I said, 'Tom, look mate, I've got

Above: Hugh Jackman making his London West End debut as Curly in the Cameron Mackintosh/National Theatre production of *Oklahoma!* at the Lyceum Theatre, London, 1999.

Opposite, above: Russell Crowe as Javert.

Opposite, centre: Tom Hooper shares his thoughts with Hugh Jackman about a scene on T Stage. Also seen are Fra Fee as Courfeyrac, Aaron Tveit, who plays Enjolras, and Killian Donnelly as Combeferre.

Opposite, bottom: Hugh Jackman, Russell Crowe and Tom Hooper share a lighter moment between takes at the dry dock in Portsmouth.

to get home to get my kids to bed.' And he was like, 'Oh, OK.' I could tell he would have kept going. But luckily it worked out."

Crowe was, indeed, in the frame but it was by no means a done deal. He had to convince the filmmakers that he could do the role and, just as importantly, he needed to convince himself. Crowe is a talented, and vastly experienced, musician and songwriter. He has recorded several albums and has toured the world with his occasional band, Thirty Odd Foot of Grunts, and with his friend, Canadian musician Alan Doyle. But *Les Misérables* was different.

"It's just not something that I knew," he said. "I knew of the show but I had never seen it. And the type of singing was just not in my field of experience. This isn't about a being a bloke who sings songs; it's a completely different form.

"I went to see the show in London and what struck me was that it was a really stirring performance and an inspiring evening at the theatre."

After seeing the stage show, he was still not convinced that he was the right man to play Javert on screen. A walk in a London park with director Tom Hooper changed everything. "After I had seen the show, I was thinking, 'It's not for me.' I was thinking of the politest way to bow out. As much as I loved it, I just felt that it wasn't for me.

"Tom and I went for a walk in Hyde Park and we started breaking the character down and we talked in depth about how he would approach the film. I was engaged intellectually and it became important to me. And it's funny, because then it switches – from them pursuing you for the role, you are now pursuing the part. I really wanted to do it."

After those initial meetings with Hooper and, later, Mackintosh and composers Claude-Michel Schönberg and Alain Boublil, they agreed to meet again, for a formal audition, later in the year.

Crowe was about to start filming *Man of Steel* and virtually every spare moment when he was not filming, he worked with voice coaches to prepare for the audition.

"One of them was Roberta Duchak and we just clicked. Roberta has had a long career as a performer and she is a gifted teacher. Hugh began working with her, too, when we started filming, so we shared her. She worked like a Trojan and never complained. I was really lucky to find Roberta and she just made it all seem possible."

Crowe, an Oscar® winner for *Gladiator*, is known for his total commitment to a role and he threw himself into the project with typical gusto while working on *Man of Steel*, part of which involved him working in a water tank. "So I had to do a lot of breathing exercises and that just fed right into what I was doing with the singing."

In September 2011, he arrived in New York for the audition that would decide if he would be part of the film. "It was on 42nd Street and Broadway, which was kind of fitting. And it was this classic Broadway rehearsal room – a piano in the corner and a little bit of space in case there were dance moves involved," he laughed. "Absolutely the kind of place where you would audition and rehearse for a musical."

He asked for a few moments to warm up and the assembled *Les Misérables* team – Hooper, Mackintosh, musical director Stephen Brooker,

Opposite: Russell Crowe as Javert leads his men through the streets of Paris in pursuit of Valjean.

Right: One of the many detailed scene designs by Eve Stewart; this one is for a shot of the convicts pulling a ship out of the sea for the song "Look Down".

Below: The prop letter sent to Inspector Javert by his superior, Monsieur Ardisson, from the Préfecture de Police telling him that he is mistaken in believing that Jean Valjean is alive.

producer Debra Hayward and the writers Schönberg and Boublil – duly trooped out while Crowe and Roberta ran through one of his favourite songs, "Old Man River".

"I've always loved that song and Roberta and I had started using it as a mood breaker while prepping the *Les Mis* songs. So I sang it and I went to the door to let them back in the rehearsal room and they all fell in like the Keystone Cops. They'd obviously been listening at the keyhole!

"I went into the audition having worked for months on two songs, 'The Confrontation'... and 'Stars' and I had never, ever sung 'Stars' properly. So I was in that room knowing that I hadn't yet sung that song properly."

Crowe also knew that there were people in the room who remained a little sceptical that he could do it justice.

"I love Claude-Michel. He had attended the session in London and given me, because I'm very sensitive, a very clear indication that he didn't believe I could scale the mountain. It wasn't anything that he said; it was just in his body language and aspect. So on the audition day, months later, I sing 'The Confrontation', and everything changed – everyone in the room was relaxed and really buoyant and happy with what they are hearing. And Claude-Michel is clearly hearing what Tom had thought he'd heard, what Cameron and Stephen thought they had heard, and now he's glowing. It was a nice feeling.

"However, then I have to sing 'Stars', this song that I'd never heard the way I wanted to hear it. But in that environment, with the belief that Tom had in me, the months of preparation, it all paid off and it just came out exactly right. I got to the notes at the end and I was flying, over the top of the notes looking down, all the sounds were being created in the same place, all the things that the other teachers and Roberta had focused on, were all there and available to me. 'Man,' I thought, 'did I get away with that or what?'"

Mackintosh and the others gathered for the audition were impressed. "Russell knew that he was taking on something risky and he wanted that. And one of the reasons we loved him so much was because he can create a completely different kind of Javert," said Mackintosh. They knew, too, that they had two great screen actors who could sing in exactly the right roles. Any thoughts of Crowe as Valjean and Jackman as Javert were over. With Crowe and Jackman – Hooper and Mackintosh's dream team – in place, the filmmakers set about casting the other leads.

CHAPTER 19

A Family Affair

Anne Hathaway, the Oscar®-nominated actress best known for *The Devil Wears Prada, One Day* and as Cat Woman in the *Batman* film, *The Dark Knight Rises*, would take the key role of Fantine and bring with her some family history.

"I've known Anne for a long time because her mother, Kathleen, was in *Les Misérables* on a national tour of America," explained Mackintosh. "And she is just perfect as Fantine."

Hathaway grew up listening to the music of *Les Misérables*. "My mother was in the national tour of *Les Mis* when I was seven," she recalled. "She was the factory girl and went on a number of times as Fantine and I got to see her. This music has been the background to my life and was such a huge part of my childhood. When I found out that I was going to play the same role that my mother played, well, it's hard to put into words how I felt. It's very personal for me. It feels like it has come a full circle in my life. I felt very lucky and the whole thing felt like serendipity."

Every single member of the cast, from the biggest Hollywood stars, such as Hugh Jackman, Russell Crowe and Anne Hathaway, to those who would be in the crowd scenes, auditioned.

"I think auditions are great," said Jackman. "Because you get to see what the dynamic will be like, and after talking with Tom at the audition I instinctively felt that he was the right choice. I actually think it's a plus to have a director that is not steeped in the musical theatre world. I think it's a plus to have someone who is more dramatically inclined.

"I knew that he would feel comfortable with recreating the period that our story is set in. I knew, too, that he would draw on Victor Hugo's novel. With a musical there are some holes in the plot and the script, but with a film you can't get away with that, and I knew that Tom would plug all of those holes. I knew that he was going to make a great piece of cinema."

When news leaked out that *Les Misérables* was casting, many of the biggest stars in Hollywood urged their agents to line up auditions.

"I found out that they were auditioning for *Les Misérables* and I kept pestering them until I got a time," said Anne Hathaway. "And because of my Mom I knew the part of Fantine so well and when I met with Tom I sang for him for about three hours. It was like a very intense work session. And then I had to wait a month until I found out that I'd got the part."

Monsieur Thénardier,
Vous remettrez Cosette à la personne.
On vous payera toutes les petites choses.
J'ai l'honneur de vous saluer avec considération,
Fantine

Above: Anne Hathaway followed in her mother's footsteps by playing the part of Fantine.

Left: Fantine's note to Monsieur Thénardier asking him to take care of her daughter Cosette.

Opposite, above: Amanda Seyfried looks pensive as the grown-up Cosette pondering on her feelings for the student Marius.

Opposite, left: Helena Bonham Carter as Madame Thénardier beneath a rather ironic notice in their inn at Montfermeil.

Opposite, right: Aaron Tveit, the American theatre and film actor as Enjolras, the leader of the Friends of the ABC group.

Amanda Seyfried, fresh from her triumph as Meryl Streep's daughter, Sophie, in the blockbuster hit *Mamma Mia!*, remembered going to see *Les Misérables* when she was a little girl. "I was ten or eleven and I saw it in Philadelphia with my parents, and it was so beautiful," she recalled. "I was playing Eponine in my head for years! *Les Misérables* is special. It means so much to so many people. I know that, because I felt the same way."

Seyfried worked intensively with a voice coach before she sent a tape to Tom Hooper and, after several auditions, won the role of Cosette. It was, she said, one of the best Christmas presents she has ever had.

"Tom rang me in December 2011 and I missed his call. I called him back and he said, 'Merry Christmas …' I said, 'What's going on?' And Tom said, 'Well, my Christmas present is that I can tell you that you've got the job.' I was thrilled. Believe me. I had to work really hard to get the part because it's very serious and I don't take it lightly. It's an honour."

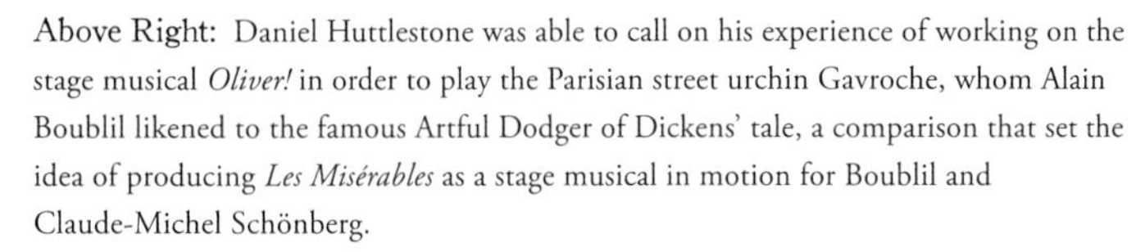

Above Right: Daniel Huttlestone was able to call on his experience of working on the stage musical *Oliver!* in order to play the Parisian street urchin Gavroche, whom Alain Boublil likened to the famous Artful Dodger of Dickens' tale, a comparison that set the idea of producing *Les Misérables* as a stage musical in motion for Boublil and Claude-Michel Schönberg.

Above left: Marius, played by Eddie Redmayne, reads a note from Cosette, whom he had met on the street and with whom he had fallen instantly in love, much to the dismay of Jean Valjean.

Below: Samantha Barks who has played Eponine in the West End as well as in the film.

Helena Bonham Carter and Sacha Baron Cohen, who had both proved their musical abilities in Tim Burton's acclaimed *Sweeney Todd: The Demon Barber of Fleet Street* as Mrs Lovett and Pirelli, would play the money-grabbing innkeepers, the Thénardiers, and Colm Wilkinson, who played the original Jean Valjean on stage in the West End, on Broadway and in Shanghai, came on board as the Bishop of Digne.

Aaron Tveit, a heartthrob in the United States thanks to his role on the hit television show *Gossip Girl* (and an experienced musical theatre performer), was cast as Enjolras: "I've been very lucky because I've done four shows on Broadway, this is my sixth movie and of course, I've done a lot of TV. There haven't been any boundaries in my career so far but *Les Misérables* is a real marriage of musical theatre and film."

Twelve-year-old Daniel Huttlestone, who played Nipper in Cameron Mackintosh's 2009 London production of *Oliver!*, with Rowan Atkinson as Fagin, landed the plum role of the street smart urchin Gavroche.

Eddie Redmayne, the young star of *My Week With Marilyn* and the acclaimed BBC World War One drama *Birdsong*, would be Marius. His love of acting started when he was at school at Eton College, where he sang in the choir, and one of his first "gigs" actually came in Cameron Mackintosh's 1994 stage production of *Oliver!*. "I was about twelve," he recalled, "and I was workhouse boy number 50. So I was one of a hundred kids but it was such a buzz. I've always loved it and I've always loved musicals, too."

Being cast in *Les Misérables* would also change lives. For Samantha Barks, *Les Misérables* would be her first film, reprising the role of Eponine that she played on the London stage for a year in 2010. The night she found out she had won the film role was one of the most memorable of her young life.

Born on the Isle of Man, Samantha came third in the BBC television talent show *I'd Do Anything*, which searched for new performers for a West End revival of *Oliver!* and featured Cameron Mackintosh as one of the judges. It launched her career and she went on to play Sally Bowles in a national tour of *Cabaret* and was starring as Nancy in *Oliver!* at Manchester's Palace Theatre on 31 January 2012, when, to her complete surprise, Mackintosh came on stage at the curtain call and announced that she would be in the film.

Above: Heather Chasen, Hugh Jackman as Valjean and Colm Wilkinson, who played Valjean in the original stage production in London in 1985, as the Bishop of Digne.

Right: Cameron Mackintosh on stage at the Palace Theatre, Manchester, telling the audience that Samantha Barks, who played Nancy in the UK tour of *Oliver!*, had been cast as Eponine in the film of *Les Misérables*.

Following pages: A panoramic shot of the film's barricade set, showing the sheer scale of the production. Eddie Redmayne, as Marius, and Amanda Seyfried, as Cosette, are visible in the centre.

"We took our bows and Cameron walked on to the stage and I wasn't thinking 'I wonder if I've got the part in the film'. No, I was thinking 'Was that a good show? Did I do my best? Did he like it?'. And then I heard him say 'Eponine' and my heart started beating faster and my mind was racing. It was like a whirlwind in my head. Then I took it in, and right there, that second, everything in my life completely changed."

Along with the other actors, such as Colm Wilkinson, Barks had an insight into both the musical theatre and film worlds, as they came together to bring *Les Misérables* to the big screen. "It was an interesting dynamic," she said. "The thing is, we weren't just filming the musical and this wasn't just another film. What made it so special was Tom's decision – a brave, bold decision – to get us all to sing live. That had never been done before and I think, really, that put everyone – those of us from the musical theatre and those great actors from the film world – in the same boat. Believe me, every day was an adventure. I'll never forget it."

As Eric Fellner put it, "I think we got very lucky. I think this was the time to make this film – when there was a bunch of actors who were right for the roles, who could all sing. I think that five years ago or in five years' time, maybe we couldn't have collected that group of actors who can sing in this way again."

Below: Cameron Mackintosh, Claude-Michel Schönberg, Michael Le Poer Trench and a huge cast manning the barricades during the filming of the finale at the Royal Naval College, Greenwich.

FRATERNITE

CHAPTER 20

Singing for Their Supper

Director Tom Hooper's decision to ask each of his actors to sing live during every single take while filming *Les Misérables* was a big risk. But it was one that paid off brilliantly.

In the past, the vast majority of musicals have all been made in the same way: the actors go into a studio to record their vocals, with full musical backing, before the cameras roll. During filming, they hear a playback of those recordings and mime along to each take. Later, in the editing suite, the filmmakers marry sound and pictures. Hooper wanted to do it differently. It was, he said, crucial to the whole project: "I became intrigued with this idea that the key to doing it was to do it live. I find with musicals on film that sometimes you don't quite believe in the reality of what you are watching.

"My theory was that if it were live, there would be a huge shift in what the genre offers. In doing my homework, I discovered that films have only ever explored live singing in a piecemeal way. Rex Harrison in *My Fair Lady* sang to a live orchestra, unlike the rest of the cast. I talked to Andy Nelson, whom I think is the pre-eminent sounder mixer of musicals in the world. He told me how Alan Parker had done *The Commitments* live.

"What hadn't been attempted before is singing live to this extent. The musical is sung-through; it's two and a half hours of live singing. The

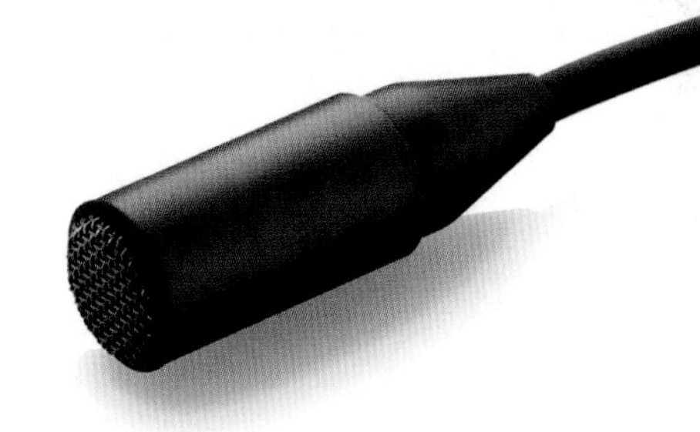

Above: One of the very small, but very sensitive microphones that were worn by the actors to record them as they sang live during the filming.

Opposite: Samantha Barks as Eponine on the barricade.

Far left: Lottie Steer takes the opportunity to try out one of the pianos used to accompany the actors as they sang on set while pianist Jennifer Whyte looks on.

Left: Anne Hathaway brilliantly conveys the despair of Fantine as she considers the situation to which she has been reduced.

Below: Eddie Redmayne and students protest.

other innovation is we decided to sing it almost entirely to live piano; this means take-to-take the tempo changes with the actors and it gives the actor the freedom of being in the moment.

"I started shooting tests with Hugh Jackman in October 2011 (five months before filming started) and it was unbelievable," said Hooper. "I screened a couple of scenes for people and what I found was that no one had any difficulty entering into the idea that this was a world where you communicate through song. Within a minute, you are in that world and you aren't struggling with suspending disbelief. It was such an exciting discovery."

Hooper discussed the practicalities of exactly how they could do it with production sound mixer Simon Hayes, re-recording sound mixer Andy Nelson and supervising music editor Gerard McCann. The result was that each actor would wear a tiny earpiece and, while singing, they would be accompanied by a pianist, playing live, out of camera shot, whom they could hear via the device.

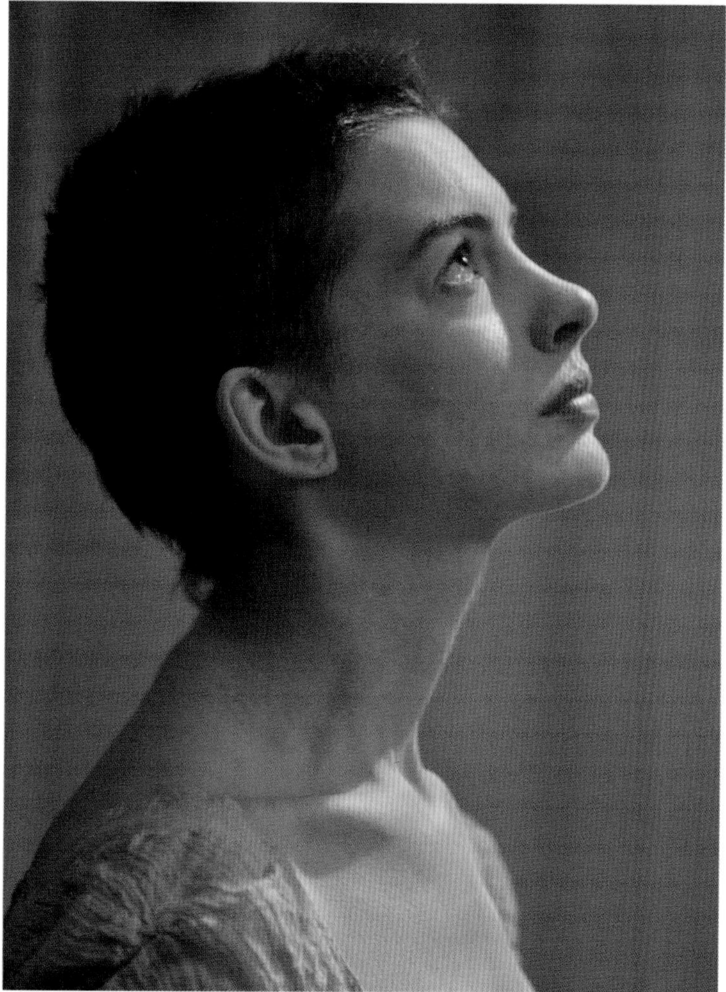

When they were filming in the studio at Pinewood, the pianists, Roger Davison and Jennifer Whyte, were in a room off the main sound stage. On location, the musicians were in a canvas tent close by.

Each of the actors was also "dressed" with a tiny microphone, hidden in their costume, which picked up their voice with recording studio clarity. "It had never been done with all the principals before and basically the technology didn't exist until very recently," said Hugh Jackman. "I was talking to Simon Hayes and he said that to get the quality of microphone you need for movie standard, this tiny thing pinned on your chest, as opposed to the big mike you would get in a recording studio, that's only existed in the last five years."

Every scene was filmed from various angles and the director required several different versions of each. That meant that the actor had to sing multiple times on different takes. Later in the editing suite, Hooper picked his favourite take of the song and the scene and then the orchestra recorded the music in a studio to fit with the action. As Tom Hooper explained, it presented particular challenges: "It means that with every take you've got to make sure that you've got all the shots you want that match the tempo because it's vey hard to cut different takes with different tempos. So I think the other thing we have done that's very unusual in musicals is to embrace the concept of the live tempo.

"When you pre-record it you have to follow decisions that you made three or four months earlier. Doing it this way, the actors can change the tempo, change the rhythm, make subtle variations so that they are really inhabiting the role and it's made it very immediate and very exciting."

Russell Crowe suspected that Hooper was about to embark on a radical approach when he arrived for his audition: "I remember I sang 'Stars' and then Tom said, 'OK, let's do it again.' So I did. And I sang it a third time, a fourth, a fifth time. And Tom was making me use my voice again and again, and although the others didn't quite know that at the time, and I didn't know at the time, stamina was a part of what he was looking for. Sometimes you'd be singing at seven in the morning and at two o'clock the following morning. Then you have to add in clarity, movement, working to the camera, being where the camera needs you to be, and, at the same time, being a hundred per cent inside the character you are playing and interpreting every one of those lines in the songs in an almost Shakespearean way. The discipline required is positively athletic."

It was a huge challenge, and all the actors, said Anne Hathaway, were a little anxious that they could sustain it. "I think we were all kind of terrified," she said. "It was one of those moments where we all bravely said 'yes' and then looked at each other and went 'what?'. But that was one of the things that was so special about this job because not only did you have to open yourself to something that you'd never done before but you're with a bunch of other actors who've never done this before and a crew that has never shot a movie like this and a director who has never done anything like this."

For Cameron Mackintosh, Hooper's decision to go live was absolutely the right one. "It brings so much to the performances," he said. "When you think about it, it is a little strange when you record your performance with an orchestra and then mime it when you are actually acting in front of a camera. You simply couldn't do that with *Les Misérables*, which is wall-to-wall music. The story is driven through the music much more than, say, *West Side Story*, which is driven through dance. I love that film, but when you watch *West Side Story* now, yes, lots of it is still thrilling, but you do get a sense that the vocals were dubbed and not as immediate as the dance.

"We were breaking new ground here. But we were blessed with Simon (Hayes) and his colleagues, who are the very best sound guys in the country. They made it work and did a fantastic job. And so did the actors. They were magnificent. When you hear Anne Hathaway sing 'I Dreamed A Dream', it takes your breath away. Hugh, Russell, Eddie, Amanda, all of them gave performances that are just beautiful."

"Some of my favourite takes are the very last ones," said Mackintosh. "When you can see that, yes, they are tired, but they have done the song so many times that they're relaxed in telling the story through the music and there is no barrier." For Tom Hooper, the decision to abandon the old ways and embrace the new was an essential, exciting part of the challenge of bringing *Les Misérables* to the screen. "We are reinventing the genre and the collective excitement of the team is not just because it's such an iconic, extraordinary piece of work, but also because we are getting this opportunity to be pioneers in a technique and that hardly ever happens. And that's a thrill."

Opposite, above: Helena Bonham Carter as Madame Thénardier enjoys the revels in her inn with her customers who include some West End theatre regulars.

Opposite, below: Anne Hathaway at the end of the film when she appears to Valjean.

Below: Eve Stewart's delicate set drawing for the scene where Little Cosette walks through the Frost Fair.

CHAPTER 21

On Set

Filming started on *Les Misérables* on 7 March, 2012 in the tiny, picturesque, mountain-top village of Gourdon in the south of France.

For three days, director Tom Hooper and his crew, along with Hugh Jackman, filmed part of the opening sequence – called a "pre-shoot" – in the beautiful backdrop of the snow capped Alps. In the story, Jean Valjean has just been released from prison after 19 long, gruelling years and embarks on his epic journey from Toulon to Paris.

Jackman embarked on a tough training regime and a strict, high protein diet to change his body shape radically to play the gaunt and muscled Valjean who has endured endless days of hard labour.

"Tom said, 'You need to be like an ox of a man, very strong, but I also want you to look worryingly thin.' And that's typical, of course, from someone who doesn't really know what it takes to get into that kind of shape," he laughed.

Jackman knew that Hooper's decision to get his actors to sing live had paid off from those very first scenes in France. "We were on a mountain top in the Alps in the South of France and it was below freezing. I could feel the cold in my voice and I *was* bloody cold," he laughed. "Tom said to me, 'When you sing live, it's immediate. Where you are becomes part of that. When you are outside, it sounds like you are outside, when you are in a church it sounds like you are in a church. It doesn't sound synthetic.' Up in that mountain I knew exactly what he meant. I was freezing cold and I felt vulnerable and you could hear that. You could see the steam coming out of my mouth."

After the short sequence filmed on location in France, Jackman had to regain the weight he had lost to play the much healthier version of Valjean in later scenes.

"So literally I was eating everything that was coming my way," he said. "I remember we were filming down in Portsmouth and [celebrity chef] Jamie Oliver has an Italian place down there and I ordered two of everything – entrées, mains, desserts. I thought, 'Oh my God, I'm going to throw up.' Then we had to drive an hour and a half to get home and by the time I was there, I was like, 'You know what? I need more food."

Anne Hathaway also underwent an extreme physical transformation for her role as Fantine. "Over five weeks I lost 25lb and I lost 15lb in the last two weeks," she said.

Fantine's journey is, in its way, as brutally hard as Valjean's long spell in prison – abandoned by her lover, forced to give up her beloved daughter Cosette in the hope she will have a better life, she ends up destitute on the streets and, in desperation, sells her teeth and her hair for money and, eventually, turns to prostitution.

"You know I'm not method, but I was playing a martyr. There's something about the depth of her suffering that gives life to the love that you experience in the rest of the film. One of the things that I loved about Victor Hugo's book is that it's an exploration of love in all its profundity, using language that is some of the most beautiful I've ever read that just ignites your heart. And then people put that to music and we get to sing it. The power of the story lies in these characters' ability to love."

Each of the actors, aware that they were in the midst of one of the most vivid, and challenging, experiences of their working lives, would offer support as one of their colleagues approached the day when they would have to sing one of their character's signature songs.

"We all had our big songs to do," said Eddie Redmayne who plays Marius. "Mine is 'Empty Chairs at Empty Tables'. And you had this gentle pressure building up, thinking 'It's me next.' Anyway, I did it and I came in the next day and Hugh said, 'Well done, mate, that was fantastic. Now, don't you feel about five inches taller?' And it's true, you do feel like this wonderful sort of weight has been lifted from your shoulders."

For Jackman, there was also the challenge of delivering a new song, "Suddenly", written for the film by Claude-Michel Schönberg and Alain Boublil and their long-time collaborator, Herbert Kretzmer.

"We were talking to Tom and he wanted to add a song with Valjean and Cosette when she is a little girl," explained Schönberg. "And we were trying to use existing music and then one day we said, 'Let's write a new song instead of trying to adapt something.'" Tom wanted to express the wonder of love that Valjean feels for Cosette when he is given charge of the little girl.

Boublil added: "And now it's an organic part of the whole show. And that's what we're most pleased about because, you know, when over 60 million people have seen the show, some of them will take any kind of change as a betrayal and we had to be very careful that it would meet their expectations."

Les Misérables was also filmed in England with Pinewood Studios as its home base. It was the first production to use the brand new sound stage – T – named after Richard Attenborough – where double Academy-Award®-nominated production designer Eve Stewart and her team recreated early nineteenth-century Parisian streets and alleyways.

Opposite, left: Hugh Jackman in contemplative mood as Jean Valjean with the village of Gourdon in the French Alps in the background.

Opposite, right: A drawing of the hilltop church by Eve Stewart where Jean Valjean finds salvation in the form of support from the Bishop of Digne.

Right, above: Cameron Mackintosh with Stephen Sondheim on the film set in 2012.

Right, below: Hugh Jackman as Valjean offers what comfort he can to Anne Hathaway as the dying Fantine, to whom he makes the promise to look after her daughter Cosette.

Following pages: Aaron Tveit as Enjolras and Eddie Redmayne as Marius view the crowd assembling outside the Café Musain.

LUNETTES
120
VINS AUTRES

SAIN

It was on T stage that the cast built a section of the famous *Les Misérables* barricade. For the film, there were two barricades. The first was "built" on set as the cameras rolled. "There's a real action side to this film," said Eddie Redmayne. "That's the way Tom likes to do things, he likes to make it real. So we had that huge set of the Paris streets, all the shops, the houses, and we had about forty students and about forty extras and five cameramen all dressed as peasants, so they could be right in amongst us, and then he said, 'Right, build a barricade. Action!' It went on for nine, ten minutes. Amazing."

The crew then built a second barricade, approximately 100 feet long and 30 feet high, at Pinewood, which was transported in sections by trucks to Greenwich, where part of the finale of the film was shot, on location.

"There was so much detail in the sets," said Anne Hathaway. "I thought Eve out did herself. You go on the sets and you really believe that people walked those streets every day. I went on to the set where we shot 'Lovely Ladies' when they were breaking it down and it's so hard to believe that it's not going to be there anymore. That's how real they felt."

The 62-day shoot was divided roughly 50–50 between Pinewood and locations in the south of England. The Royal Naval base at Portsmouth, home of the oldest dry dock in the world, doubled as Toulon port and provided the backdrop of the opening scene where unfortunate inmates of the brutally harsh Bagne Prison, including Valjean, are put to work. Some 30 miles away, Winchester College, the famous public school founded in 1382, became a French convent where Valjean and Cosette seek refuge. Greenwich Naval College and the surrounding area became the Place de la Bastille in Paris with hundreds of extras running through the surrounding streets as revolutionary students. While the historic dockyard in Chatham, Kent, became the location for various scenes, including Valjean's factory in Montreuil-sur-Mer where he meets the unfortunate Fantine.

Hooper wanted his actors to look the part and that meant actors playing street urchins and the desperately poor would be grimy and dirty. "A lot of people had to wear plastic moulds on their teeth that were painted to look grimy. I was lucky, I didn't." recalled Anne Hathaway.

She did, though, have her beautiful, black flowing tresses shorn off in front of the camera for the scene where Fantine sells her hair for money and the tears flowed for real. "I wasn't expecting it to be such a big deal because it was my idea," she recalled later, "something I wanted to do for a long time and I knew that it was something that the character did, so I just offered it to the director, and he said 'yes' and as it got closer, I just thought, 'I can't really take it back now.' I've now done back flips out of windows, I've jumped off of buildings, but cutting off my hair reduced me to a mental-patient level of crying. I was inconsolable."

It was, though, representative of the cast's commitment to the cause and Hooper's desire to make the film as realistic as possible. During the street scenes, for example, Hooper would have as many as five of his crew, all dressed in period costume, with hand-held cameras in the thick of the action.

"It was unlike anything I'd ever done before," said Aaron Tveit. "We wouldn't start and stop, doing little bits of the scene, we would do chunks of five, six minutes and the cameramen were all dressed in period costumes

“Suddenly”

Suddenly you’re here
Suddenly it starts
Can two anxious hearts
Beat as one?
Yesterday I was alone
Today you are beside me
Something still unclear
Something not yet here
Has begun.

Suddenly the world
Seems a different place
Somehow full of grace
Full of light
How was I to know
That so much hope
Was held inside me?
What is past is gone
Now we journey on
Through the night.

and in there with us with their cameras covered up. It was this neat, interactive experience.”

Russell Crowe has worked with some of the best film directors in the business, including Sir Ridley Scott, Ron Howard, Peter Weir, Michael Mann and Darren Aronofsky. He rates Hooper alongside those giants.

“Tom’s style, from what I was picking up from observing his way of directing, borrows a little bit from [Stanley] Kubrick in that his frames take in the entire world, so you don’t get a respite from the world that you are in. When he’s in your face, he’s in your face. And if he wants to have a close-up, that camera is right in front of you, like eight or ten inches from your head. That was his process – he wanted to take people on the journey by taking them into this universe.”

Opposite: The members of the Friends of the ABC, who include Hugh Skinner (Joly), Eddie Redmayne (Marius), Jamie Muscato (Student), Aaron Tveit (Enjolras) and George Blagden (Grantaire).

Above left: The first two verses of the lyrics of “Suddenly” by Alain Boublil and Herbert Kretzmer, which was created especially for Jean Valjean to sing in the movie.

Above right: A scene design by Eve Stewart for the Parisian slums.

Below: Crew and technicians prepare the set created on T Stage at Pinewood Studios. Bernard Bellew (Co-producer) is seen to the right of the yellow ladder, while Danny Cohen (Director of Photography) talks to Tom Hooper (bottom right).

CHAPTER 22

The Power of *Les Misérables*

When filming finally wrapped on *Les Misérables* in June 2012, the cast were left to reflect on what they had accomplished. "I have to say it was the most fully absorbing experience right from the time of the auditions, working with the voice coach, rehearsals through to, and including, doing the movie itself," said Russell Crowe. "There's part of me that, in the future, whenever I'm starting a movie I'll wish that I was starting *Les Misérables* again. That's how big that experience was."

Hugh Jackman agreed. It was, said Jackman, quite unlike anything he had done before and he cherished being part of "the team" that brought *Les Misérables*, the musical, to a worldwide cinema audience.

"Musicals are the Mount Everest of filmmaking," he said. "Musical films are the hardest to pull off and get right and when they don't work, they are the worst thing known to man. You can't rely on the fact that if a musical has been a big hit on stage that the movie will be a big hit, too. You can't rest on those laurels. Tom Hooper knew that. He knew that he had to make people love this movie in its own right. And he honoured the story in the best possible way."

What is, then, the enduring power of *Les Misérables*?

"For me, *Les Misérables* is about finding the best in the human spirit," said Jackman. "Every character in this story has major obstacles, bigger than most of us encounter in life, and you see them under duress doing their utmost to find the best in themselves. We can relate to that and that's why it's so uplifting. They fail and they try again. Valjean, whom I suppose is the hero in this, fails and gets a second chance, a third chance and when he gets those

Opposite, above: Jean Valjean sits at one of the benches in the jet-bead factory in Montreuil-sur-Mer, which he acquired after his redemption led to him turning over a new leaf and making his fortune. As fate would have it, it is also the factory where Fantine works before being unfairly dismissed.

Left: Hugh Jackman was surely not the only one impressed by Russell Crowe's abilities to handle a horse during filming.

Opposite, below: Anne Hathaway and Tom Hooper relax between takes.

chances he makes the most of them; he battles all the time. And I think, even though it's called *Les Misérables*, that's why it's such an uplifting story."

Jackman had known Crowe for many years, stretching back to the days when they were both young actors starting out in Australia, but they had never worked together before *Les Misérables*. "I think Russell did a fantastic job," he said. "I remember doing a scene in Greenwich where he's on horseback chasing me, as Valjean, at full gallop. It's a big action scene, really technical, and it calls for brilliant riding skills. And he nailed it every time."

Jackman had also sung with Anne Hathaway at the Oscars® in 2009 when Jackman was hosting the show. When Hathaway hosted the Oscars® in 2011, she serenaded Jackman with a specially re-written version of "On My Own". Tom Hooper witnessed it and remembered thinking, "Were they doing some kind of subtle or not-so-subtle pitch … [and] was that the most extraordinary attempt to manipulate me into saying 'Hello, Anne Hathaway and Hugh Jackman – maybe that makes sense'? I have joked about this with Annie and she smiled modestly."

"I knew Anne had a great voice," said Jackman, "and I heard Tom describe her as the muse of the production and I think that's true. I remember when we were doing rehearsals and you could have filmed her then and there with a script in her hand. She … was totally believable in every way."

Singing "I Dreamed A Dream" was, of course, a big moment for the young actress. Her extraordinarily powerful, beautifully moving performance is loaded with pathos and caused a sensation when it was used as the soundtrack to the trailer that gave fans a tantalising glimpse of what to expect from Hooper's bold film.

"I knew the song backwards and forwards and then you start to apply the reality of the scene," she said. "And the reality of the scene is that she is devastated. She has just become a prostitute and she's processing that. The song comes in a different place in the movie. In the show, it's just after she's been fired from the factory so there's still a little hope in it. In the movie, she's literally at the bottom of a hole and realizing that she's never going to get out of it.

"It started to affect my voice. I started to think, 'I can't sing this pretty because it will take the audience out of the moment.' It seemed selfish to go for the pretty version of it, so I just decided to apply the truth to the melody to see what would happen. I didn't really know what I was going to do before I did it. Actually, it turned into a little bit of an out-of-body experience. It was scary to bring this rawness to a song that has been sung by some of the greatest singers who have ever lived. But I had so much support from Tom, Cameron and Claude-Michel and Alain, so we just went for it and said, 'OK, this is the film version and now it exists and that's that.'"

Each of the cast would say that the film was demanding but ultimately rewarding. Hooper's ground-breaking approach with the actors singing live paid off. "I have to say *Mamma Mia!* was a piece of cake compared to this," noted Amanda Seyfried. "*Mamma Mia!* was hard, but we pre-recorded all the songs, and also I was singing pop music, which is a dream compared to this. This is classical and it's so much harder. But I also have to say it was just so thrilling and so much more rewarding. And you know, everybody was so supportive. There was just this feeling that we were all in it together. We all helped each other do the very best we could."

Russell Crowe agreed: "During filming everyone was connected, even if you weren't there on a certain day, you would hear things like 'Amanda was amazing, they were all crying during her performance', or 'Samantha is a superstar, she has the set entranced', or you'd hear the girls giggling over the beauty of Eddie or Aaron's tone. There was a great vibe. Everybody was doing their best and it was a really cohesive feeling in the cast, just like you would get in a theatre show."

Cameron Mackintosh was on set almost every day during filming. He was clearly delighted as *Les Misérables* the movie was brought so vividly to life.

"All I can say is that I don't think anyone will have ever seen a musical as a film like this. It's a completely different style. Although parts of it are heightened because it is a musical, it feels very real and the level of detail in the world that Tom has created is staggering. You can see the paint peeling on the hulls of the ships, you can smell the seaweed and, most important of all, you can hear the emotion in the voices of these extraordinary actors and become lost in the power of their performances."

Above: Helena Bonham Carter poses in Madame Thénardier's wedding guest finery on location.

Right: Amanda Seyfried and Eddie Redmayne film a scene from Cosette and Marius's wedding day.

For Crowe, the credit goes to Tom Hooper and his vision, drive and determination to make *Les Misérables* a unique cinematic experience.

"You can imagine the pressure Tom was under because it was a massive task, and he didn't take any of the easy options," said Crowe. "He had a studio and all those corporate responsibilities to deal with, he had the production company, Working Title, and he had twenty-seven years of record breaking theatrical history to live up to.

"He had Cameron, Claude-Michel, Alain, people who have been passionate about this thing all that time, who know where every single crotchet and quaver should be. So he had to deal with all of that. But the communication was continuous and nobody got in the way of the progress Tom was making with his movie. I think that attitude from Tom and the producers filtered down to the performers because everybody stood their ground and did their job. And that was the very cool thing about it.

"I loved watching Cameron's face every day when he was on set, when he saw things created before his eyes that he could never have imagined. You know, the opening of the film is so epic and so bold and Cameron was standing with me in Portsmouth, looking across this vast, vast set, and he said, 'I'd never imagined it to be this, but I'll never ever be able to hear this music again without seeing this ...'"

Left: Cameron Mackintosh smiles down from the top of the barricade after the successful completion of filming at Pinewood.

Below: Tom Hooper explains what he needs from the cast and crew during filming in Greenwich in east London.

Les Misérables Film Awards

84 WINS AND 172 NOMINATIONS

UK

BAFTA FILM AWARDS, 2013

Best Supporting Actress - Anne Hathaway (Fantine)
Best Production Design - Eve Stewart, Anna Lynch-Robinson
Best Make Up/Hair - Lisa Westcott, Julie Dartnell
Best Sound - John Warhurst, Jonathan Allen, Lee Walpole, Mark Paterson, Simon Hayes, Andy Nelson

EMPIRE AWARDS, 2013

Best Female Newcomer – Samantha Barks (Eponine)

LONDON CRITICS CIRCLE FILM AWARDS, 2013

Supporting Actress of the Year - Anne Hathaway (Fantine)

US

ACADEMY AWARDS, 2013

Best Performance by an Actress in a Supporting Role - Anne Hathaway (Fantine)
Best Achievement in Makeup and Hairstyling - Lisa Westcott, Julie Dartnell
Best Achievement in Sound Mixing - Andy Nelson, Mark Paterson, Simon Hayes

GOLDEN GLOBES, 2013

Best Motion Picture - Comedy or Musical
Best Performance by an Actor in a Motion Picture - Comedy or Musical - Hugh Jackman (Jean Valjean)
Best Performance by an Actress in a Supporting Role in a Motion Picture - Anne Hathaway (Fantine)

SCREEN ACTORS GUILD AWARDS, 2013

Outstanding Performance by a Female Actor in a Supporting Role - Anne Hathaway (Fantine)

ACADEMY OF SCIENCE FICTION, FANTASY & HORROR FILMS (SATURN AWARD), 2013

Best Costumes - Paco Delgado

AFI AWARDS, 2013

Movie of the Year

AFRICAN-AMERICAN FILM CRITICS ASSOCIATION (AAFCA) AWARDS, 2012

Top 10 Films (6th Place)

ALLIANCE OF WOMEN FILM JOURNALISTS (EDA), 2013

Best Supporting Actress - Anne Hathaway (Fantine)
Special Mention Award - Unforgettable Moment - For the scene where Fantine sings "I Dreamed a Dream".

ASCAP FILM AND TELEVISION MUSIC AWARDS, 2013

Top Box Office Films - Claude-Michel Schönberg, Alain Boublil, Herbert Kretzmer

AUSTIN FILM CRITICS ASSOCIATION, 2012

Best Supporting Actress - Anne Hathaway (Fantine)

AWARDS CIRCUIT COMMUNITY AWARDS, 2012

Best Actress in a Supporting Role - Anne Hathaway (Fantine)
Best Motion Picture - Tim Bevan, Eric Fellner, Debra Hayward, Cameron Mackintosh
Best Production Design - Eve Stewart, Anna Lynch-Robinson
Best Sound
Best Cast Ensemble - Isabelle Allen, Samantha Barks, Helena Bonham Carter, Sacha Baron Cohen, Russell Crowe, Anne Hathaway, Daniel Huttlestone, Hugh Jackman, Eddie Redmayne, Amanda Seyfried, Aaron Tveit, Colm Wilkinson

BLACK FILM CRITICS CIRCLE AWARDS, 2012

Best Supporting Actress - Anne Hathaway (Fantine)

BOSTON ONLINE FILM CRITICS ASSOCIATION, 2012

Best Supporting Actress - Anne Hathaway (Fantine)

BROADCAST FILM CRITICS ASSOCIATION AWARDS (CRITICS CHOICE AWARD), 2013

Best Supporting Actress - Anne Hathaway (Fantine)

CENTRAL OHIO FILM CRITICS ASSOCIATION, 2013

Best Supporting Actress - Anne Hathaway (Fantine)

CHRISTOPHER AWARDS, 2013

Feature Films - Tom Hooper (director), William Nicholson (writer), Alain Boublil (writer), Claude-Michel Schönberg (writer), Herbert Kretzmer (writer), Cameron Mackintosh (producer), Tim Bevan (producer), Eric Fellner (producer), Debra Hayward (producer), Bernard Bellew (co-producer), Nicholas Allott (executive producer), Liza Chasin (executive producer), Angela Morrison (executive producer), F. Richard Pappas (executive producer), Working Title Films (production company), Universal Pictures (production company), Cameron Mackintosh Ltd. (production company)

CINEMA AUDIO SOCIETY, 2013

Outstanding Achievement in Sound Mixing for Motion Pictures - Live Action - Simon Hayes (production mixer), Andy Nelson (re-recording mixer), Mark Paterson (re-recording mixer), Jonathan Allen (scoring mixer), Robert Edwards (adr mixer), Pete Smith (foley mixer)

DENVER FILM CRITICS SOCIETY, 2013

Best Supporting Actress - Anne Hathaway (Fantine)

DETROIT FILM CRITICS SOCIETY, 2012

Best Supporting Actress - Anne Hathaway (Fantine)

FLORIDA FILM CRITICS CIRCLE AWARDS, 2012

Best Supporting Actress - Anne Hathaway (Fantine)

GAY AND LESBIAN ENTERTAINMENT CRITICS ASSOCIATION (GALECA), 2013

Film Performance of the Year – Actress - Anne Hathaway (Fantine)

GOLD DERBY AWARDS, 2013

Supporting Actress - Anne Hathaway (Fantine)

Makeup/Hair - Lisa Westcott, Julie Dartnell
Sound - Andy Nelson, Mark Paterson, Simon Hayes, Lee Walpole, John Warhurst

GOLDEN SCHMOES AWARD, 2012

Best Supporting Actress of the Year - Anne Hathaway (Fantine)

GOLDEN TRAILER AWARDS, 2013

Best Music - Universal Pictures Seismic Productions For "I Dreamed a Dream".

HOLLYWOOD FILM AWARDS, 2012

Hollywood Discovery Award Best Trailer - To Erin Wyatt.
Producer of the Year - Tim Bevan, Eric Fellner, Debra Hayward, Cameron Mackintosh
Spotlight Award - Samantha Barks (Eponine)

HOUSTON FILM CRITICS SOCIETY AWARDS, 2012

Best Supporting Actress - Anne Hathaway (Fantine)

IGN SUMMER MOVIE AWARDS, 2012

People's Choice Award, Best Movie Actress - Anne Hathaway (Fantine)

INDIANA FILM JOURNALISTS ASSOCIATION, 2012

Best Supporting Actress - Anne Hathaway (Fantine)

IOWA FILM CRITICS AWARDS, 2013

Best Supporting Actress - Anne Hathaway (Fantine)

KANSAS CITY FILM CRITICS CIRCLE AWARDS, 2013

Best Supporting Actress - Anne Hathaway (Fantine)

LAS VEGAS FILM CRITICS SOCIETY AWARDS, 2012

Best Supporting Actress - Anne Hathaway (Fantine)

MOTION PICTURE SOUND EDITORS USA (GOLDEN REEL AWARD), 2013

Best Sound Editing - Music in a Musical Feature Film - Alastair Sirkett (vocals editor), Gerard McCann (supervising music editor), Robert Houston (music editor), John Warhurst (co-supervising/vocals editor), Rael Jones (music editor), Tim Hands (vocals editor), James Bellamy (music editor)

MOVIEGUIDE AWARDS, 2013

Epiphany Prize Most Inspiring Movie

NATIONAL BOARD OF REVIEW, 2013

Top Films
Best Acting by an Ensemble - Hugh Jackman, Russell Crowe, Anne Hathaway, Amanda Seyfried, Eddie Redmayne, Samantha Barks, Aaron Tveit, Sacha Baron Cohen, Helena Bonham Carter, Colm Wilkinson, Isabelle Allen, Natalya Angel Wallace, Daniel Huttlestone

NEVADA FILM CRITICS SOCIETY, 2012

Best Production Design – Eve Stewart

NEW YORK FILM CRITICS ONLINE, 2012

Best Supporting Actress - Anne Hathaway
Top Films of the Year

NORTH CAROLINA FILM CRITICS ASSOCIATION, 2013

Best Supporting Actress - Anne Hathaway (Fantine)

NORTH TEXAS FILM CRITICS ASSOCIATION, 2013

Best Supporting Actress - Anne Hathaway (Fantine)

OKLAHOMA FILM CRITICS CIRCLE AWARDS, 2012

Best Supporting Actress - Anne Hathaway (Fantine)

ONLINE FILM & TELEVISION ASSOCIATION, 2013

Best Supporting Actress - Anne Hathaway
Best Breakthrough Performance: Male - Eddie Redmayne
Best Music, Adapted Song - Claude-Michel Schönberg, Alain Boublil, Herbert Kretzmer, Anne Hathaway for the song "I Dreamed a Dream".
Best Sound Mixing - Simon Hayes, Andy Nelson, Mark Paterson
Best Movie Trailer - For the first theatrical trailer featuring Anne Hathaway's version of the classic ballad "I Dreamed a Dream".

ONLINE FILM CRITICS SOCIETY AWARDS, 2013

Best Supporting Actress - Anne Hathaway (Fantine)

PALM SPRINGS INTERNATIONAL FILM FESTIVAL, 2013

Sonny Bono Visionary Award – Tom Hooper

PHOENIX FILM CRITICS SOCIETY AWARDS, 2012

Best Actress in a Supporting Role – Anne Hathaway (Fantine)

SANTA BARBARA INTERNATIONAL FILM FESTIVAL, 2013

Virtuoso Award - Eddie Redmayne (Marius)

SATELLITE AWARDS, 2012

Best Sound (Editing & Mixing) - Andy Nelson, John Warhurst, Lee Walpole, Simon Hayes
Best Original Song - Hugh Jackman, Claude-Michel Schönberg, Alain Boublil, Herbert Kretzmer -"Suddenly"
Best Actress in a Supporting Role - Anne Hathaway
Special Achievement Award Best Ensemble, Motion Picture - Hugh Jackman, Russell Crowe, Anne Hathaway, Amanda Seyfried, Eddie Redmayne, Samantha Barks, Helena Bonham Carter, Sacha Baron Cohen, Aaron Tveit, Daniel Huttlestone, Isabelle Allen, Natalya Angel Wallace, Colm Wilkinson

SOUTHEASTERN FILM CRITICS ASSOCIATION AWARDS, 2012

Best Supporting Actress - Anne Hathaway (Fantine)

UTAH FILM CRITICS ASSOCIATION AWARDS, 2012

Best Supporting Actress - Anne Hathaway (Fantine)

WASHINGTON DC AREA FILM CRITICS ASSOCIATION AWARDS, 2012

Best Ensemble
Best Supporting Actress - Anne Hathaway (Fantine)

WOMEN FILM CRITICS CIRCLE AWARDS, 2012

Mommie Dearest Worst Screen Mom of the Year Award - Helena Bonham Carter (Mme Thénardier)
Best Actress – Anne Hathaway (Fantine)

YOUNG ARTIST AWARDS, 2013

Best Performance in a Feature Film - Supporting Young Actress Ten and Under – Isabelle Allen (Cosette)

WORLD

ITALIAN ONLINE MOVIE AWARDS (IOMA), 2013

Best Supporting Actress (Miglior attrice non protagonista) - Anne Hathaway (Fantine)

AWARDS OF THE JAPANESE ACADEMY, 2014

Best Foreign Language Film

NIKKAN SPORTS FILM AWARDS, 2013

Best Foreign Film - Tom Hooper

KOFRA FILM AWARDS, 2013

Best Foreign Film

GLOBAL NONVIOLENT FILM FESTIVAL, 2014

Cinematography - Danny Cohen

Top: Anne Hathaway poses, beaming, with her Academy Award for Best Supporting Actress.

Opposite: Helena Bonham Carter, Sacha Baron Cohen, Amanda Seyfried, Eddie Redmayne, Anne Hathaway and Hugh Jackman celebrate *Les Misérables'* win for Best Motion Picture - Comedy or Musical, at the Golden Globes.

Above: Poster advertising the film premiere in Japan.

CHAPTER 23

Tomorrow Will Always Come

With the film an Oscar-winning success, *Les Misérables* asserted its stage primacy afresh, via the global roll-out of the new 25th-anniversary production alongside the ever-increasing sense of Victor Hugo's story transcending time and place.

For many theatre productions, the film can be the end stop. By contrast the film of *Les Misérables* managed to bring a huge new international audience to a show that was not only still running but also, since 2009, has had two spectacularly different stagings. No other show in history has had two lives during a continuous run that has no end in sight.

But while the original production at the Queen's Theatre has continued to play to 95% capacity, the reinvented *Les Misérables* widened its reach, prompting amongst others, a return to Broadway's Imperial Theatre. "This *Les Miz* will give the musical's fans a chance to assess how a new generation of performers meets the challenges of the score", wrote the *New York Times*. A history-making run at the newly-opened Dubai Opera touched chords in an area of the world that had not seen the show before, "Dirty politics, murky morality and a disenfranchised society crushed by authoritarianism. It's been two centuries since *Les Misérables* tackled these themes. When will we stop being able to relate?" wrote *Gulf News*. Carrie Hope Fletcher, who played Eponine later reflected, "We had no idea how the audiences would respond to *Les Mis* as Dubai has a very different culture to the UK, and we obviously needed to respect that. How would things land, would certain things need to be changed or toned down, like Lovely Ladies? But audiences were on their feet every night. There was a real sense of appreciation and gratitude that we'd taken the show out there." Transporting the show to Mexico City, where the Teatro Telcel is six floors below street level, provided the technical team with challenges of a different kind. "The scenery all had to be lowered 21 metres and loaded in through the steel grid above the stage. It was the first time we had ever had to do that." said the production manager Chris Boone. A feat which surely gives new meaning to the musical's rousing question, "Do you hear the people sing?".

Familiarity bred contentment, not contempt. "Three-and-a-half stars the last time. Four now," wrote Chris Jones in the *Chicago Tribune* of a return visit to the Windy City in October 2017. Jones was among those to invoke *Hamilton* by way of comparison: a contemporary success story whose creator,

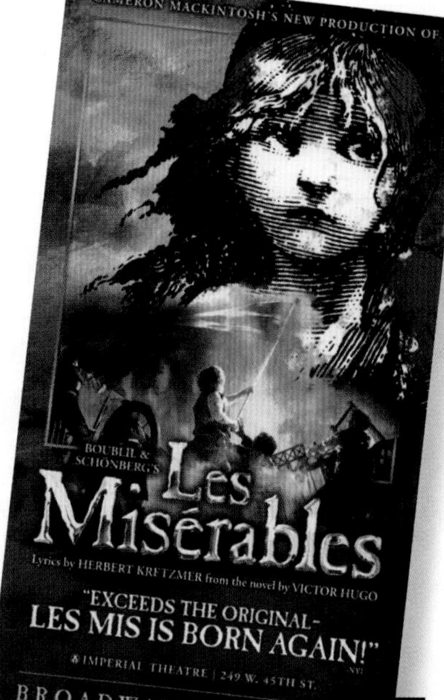

Right: Leaflet for the 25th Anniversary production on Broadway, 2014.

Below: Simon Gleeson as the convict Jean Valjean, Melbourne, 2014.

Opposite, top: "Look Down", 25th Anniversary production, UK Tour, 2010.

Opposite below: Patrice Tipoki as Fantine, Melbourne, 2014.

Opposite, background: Matt Kinley's original design for the factory exterior for the 25th anniversary production, 2010.

Lin-Manuel Miranda, has long cited *Les Mis* as a much-admired and crucial inspiration in his own work.

The legendary British film director Alfred Hitchcock was the first to predict of *Les Misérables*, "That book would make a great musical" – he was certainly proved right. The show resonates the world over, demonstrating its encompassing appeal – a 30th anniversary tour in Japan confirmed that country's affection for it across the years (the Japanese booked the original production within six weeks of its London premiere); it revisited Korea, where the film had become their highest grossing musical of all time and where audiences had first flocked to the new production in 2012. The American tours to this day reap astonishing grosses across the country – a testament to the musical's ongoing appeal well away from its East Coast beginnings in Washington and New York.

Casting has continued to celebrate the spirit of coming together and inclusion that are inbuilt in the material. Eva Noblezada, Rachelle Ann Go, and Jeon Na-Young, the first Asian to perform the role of Fantine in the West End, are among those *Les Mis* performers, originating from the Far East, who testify to the show's broad reach. The much-admired Norm Lewis played Javert at multiple points, including the gala O2 concert in 2010, while another African-American, Lawrence Clayton, was Valjean in the "splendidly reworked" (*New York Times*) American premiere of the 25th-anniversary production, which bowed at the Paper Mill Playhouse in New Jersey in December that year. Connor, the director, spoke of Clayton's Jean Valjean adding an edge to lines in which the ex-convict describes having been chained like a slave: "And when he sang the prayer 'Bring Him Home', it broke your heart to hear it sung in that soulful way." Olivier nominee Kyle Scatliffe brought fervour and authority to Enjolras on Broadway in 2014 and became something of a matinee idol.

No less impressive remains the extent to which the show allows cast members to move with it from one theatre capital to another (Colm Wilkinson remains the defining example there) and also draws performers back, like moths to some irresistible musical flame. Alfie Boe and John Owen-Jones both followed in Karimloo's New York footsteps as Jean Valjean, while Karimloo preceded his Broadway triumph in the role with occupancy of the same star part in Toronto and London. His youthfulness clearly striking a chord with the ever-enlarging audience of young people who claim the musical afresh as their own. "Too often musicals get older with their audience, but in this case we are the only ones who get older while, onstage, Cosette, Marius, the students' revolt, and their ideas are still young as ever", said Alain Boublil and Claude-Michel Schönberg.

Among Karimloo's Broadway admirers was his friend, Irishman Killian Donnelly, who has himself graduated through the ranks from the ensemble to play the role in the West End and head the 2018-2019 UK and Ireland tour. "I absolutely can't wait. The last Irish person to play Valjean in Dublin was the legend that is Colm Wilkinson and he originated the role, so I have big shoes to fill," he said. Alistair Brammer, too, began his *Les Mis* –related ascent by appearing in a school edition before going on to play Marius and then appear as the student Prouvaire in the film.

Accolades pour in, bringing the awards tally over the years to 160 and climbing. The website-driven Whatsonstage prizes in London have honoured

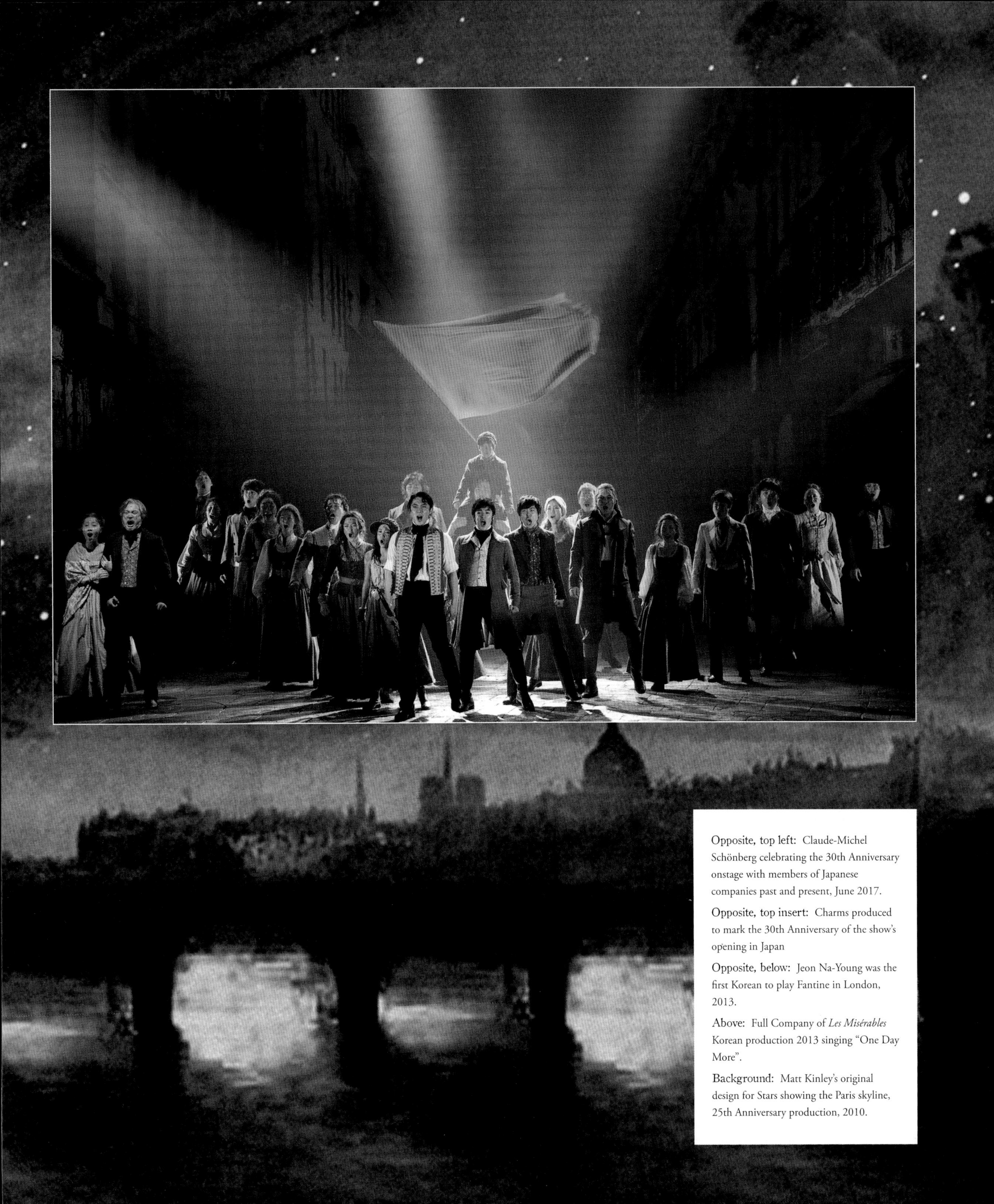

Opposite, top left: Claude-Michel Schönberg celebrating the 30th Anniversary onstage with members of Japanese companies past and present, June 2017.

Opposite, top insert: Charms produced to mark the 30th Anniversary of the show's opening in Japan

Opposite, below: Jeon Na-Young was the first Korean to play Fantine in London, 2013.

Above: Full Company of *Les Misérables* Korean production 2013 singing "One Day More".

Background: Matt Kinley's original design for Stars showing the Paris skyline, 25th Anniversary production, 2010.

the musical more or less annually in recent years, ranging from three consecutive nods for Takeover in a Role (Boe and Karimloo included) to two for West End Show and a further one for Original Cast Recording. The 25th Anniversary Australian production won five 2015 Helpmann Awards in a country whose *Les Misérables* tour opened in Melbourne, where the State Library of Victoria recognised the production with a major exhibition packed full of remarkable loans from halfway across the globe. Among the highlights of *Victor Hugo: Les Misérables – From Page to Stage* was the first-ever showing of Hugo's original 945-page manuscript outside Europe – a travelling treasure if there ever was one.

Some awards wouldn't have been possible at the time of the show's London and New York bows, among them a 2015 prize for Best Twitter Engagement for @lesmisofficial. But social media is now embedded in our lives, not least with regard to a show whose ever-evolving fan base seeks out up to the minute avenues for communication. As Mackintosh says "It is the new word of mouth." Jon Kennedy, Mackintosh's Social Media Manager, points to a Facebook page with over 1.5 million likes and more than 31,000 5-star reviews. Factor in posts reaching over 2 million people on average per month, more than 150,000 Twitter followers, and 50,000-plus accounts reached monthly via Instagram. You have an array of channels, says Kennedy, "that are fresh and interesting to our audience, especially as so many have seen the show countless times and know it line-for-line". Flash mobs utilising the score to address matters ranging from speech day at school to presidential impeachment draw upon the ever-expanding resources of social media.

Inevitably with a show of this special vintage anniversaries play an ongoing role, the 30th anniversary gala in aid of the Save the Children Syria Children's Appeal held at Queen's Theatre on 8 October 2015 had a finale bringing together Colm Wilkinson and Roger Allam – London's original Valjean and Javert – alongside Alfie Boe, John Owen-Jones, Geronimo Rauch, Patti LuPone and Frances Ruffelle. The show's future was represented by 130 children from a production at the Cardiff Millennium Centre who lined the aisles of the theatre as they sang acapella 'Do You Hear the People Sing'?. For all of them it was a night in the West End they will never forget and for some it may have sown the seeds of their future career.

What, then, of its future, beyond adding to the galloping tally of performances and noting the seamless dovetailing of two distinct but complementary productions? "There's always something around the corner for *Les Mis*," or so says Mackintosh, who admits to "people continually

Top: Hayden Tee as Javert and Simon Gleeson as Valjean confront each other following the death of Fantine, Melbourne, 2014.

Middle: Her Majesty's Theatre, Melbourne on the opening night of the 25th Anniversary production tour, 3 July 2014.

Below: Leaflet promoting educational activities in association with the *Les Misérables From Page to Stage* exhibition at the State Library of Victoria, Melbourne, 2014.

Opposite, top right: Matt Shingledecker as Enjolras rallies the students in the ABC Café, US Tour, 2018.

Opposite, below: Anthony Crane as Thénardier, US Tour, 2018.

Background: Design by Matt Kinley for Valjean's factory in Montreuil-Sur-Mer.

DON'T WAIT
ONE DAY MORE.

Les
Misérables

BROADWAY'S IMPERIAL THEATRE 249 West 45th Street
TELECHARGE.COM | 212.239.6200 | LesMiz.com/Broadway

Left: Poster featuring Kyle Scatliffe as Enjolras, Broadway, 2014.

Right: Killian Donnelly as Valjean and Zoe Simon as Little Cosette. Promotional shot for the UK Tour, autumn 2018.

Insert right: "30 years and counting" card with 30 Cosette logos to celebrate the show's 30th Birthday, London, 8 October 2015.

Far right: #Love Les Mis – some example responses to the show on social media, 2016.

Far right, insert: Award certificate for Best Twitter Engagement won by Les Misérables, 2015

Far right, insert: Leaflet for the production celebrating 30 years in London, October 2015.

Below: Cast members past and present reunited on stage for the 30th Anniversary of *Les Misérables* together with 130 schoolchildren from Wales who sang "Do You Hear the People Sing?" from the aisles of Queen's Theatre, London, 8 October 2015.

Background: Design by Matt Kinley for the docks at Digne.

#LOVELESMIS
Fans tell us why they #LoveLesMis on our award-winning social media platforms
#LoveLesMis When in doubt, Les Mis it out
@ThatSequoyaGirl
I #LoveLesMis because it is the best show ever! Can't wait to see it for the 50th time!
@ShentonStage
'Les Mis never leaves you, it stays in your heart forever'
- Samantha Barks
#LoveLesMis AMAZING!!!!!
@Rory-Woop
I #LoveLesMis as it captures the compexity and imact of the novel
@AnnaMoloney1
I #LoveLesMis because it shows a happy ending for people who have been through so much
@nadiaahamed
#LoveLesMis This is the greatest thing of all time
@EhrenSchult
#LoveLesMis everything about it blows you away... The actors, the emotion behind the show and of course the music
@ChloexCharlotte
What makes the s
www.lesmis.com
lesmis
ALSO RECOGNISED AWARDS 2015
Best Twitter Engagement
WINNER
Les Misérables
for @Lesmisofficial
at the Queen's Theatre
Terri Paddock & Mark Shenton
Founders
MyTheatreMates.com
MY THEATRE MATES
30 YEARS AND COUNTING!
BARBICAN THEATRE
8 • 10 • 1985
QUEEN'S THEATRE
8 • 10 • 2015
Les Misérables
CELEBRATING 30 YEARS OF THE STUNNING ORIGINAL
QUEEN'S THEATRE
ONE DECADE MORE!
30TH ANNIVERSARY
Les Misérables
30TH ANNIVERSARY 8TH OCTOBER 2015

approaching me with new ways of seeing and experiencing *Les Mis*; we love people coming to us with new versions. If we don't think it's in the spirit of the piece, we will say so, but as with any great piece of writing, this show survives most things."

Surely just as rewarding as the history-making statistics is to reflect upon the affective breadth and sweep of a show that for reasons no one could have foreseen clearly keeps on giving and now has a freshly energised production to respond to its insatiable audience. "There's something you can take away from the show, no matter where you are in your personal life," says Killian Donnelly. Herbert Kretzmer, the musical's lyricist, has pointed to "the universality of Victor Hugo's human portraits and mighty themes. There's an Inspector Javert in police forces everywhere – incorruptible and implacable. There are Valjeans everywhere, too, but never enough of them. The inner cities of the world are awash with disappointed drifters like Fantine, lost in their unfathomable problems. The characters of *Les Misérables* are common to all races, recognizable everywhere in their deep humanity as well as their guile."

So, where does this leave a self-described "musical phenomenon" that the show's creators, regardless of their age, are well aware could outlive both them and many a *Les Misérables* playgoer? "I know the show will outlive me," says Mackintosh, "and it's now quite likely that it will outlive me in its endless London run." Few could have anticipated as much prior to an English-language debut that, from the pulsating musical surge of its first minutes onward, sweeps playgoers along on a journey. That journey stands apart from the individual tastes and fashions of the age to tap into a timeless appeal to the possibilities of human endeavour and betterment and to a defining generosity of spirit. Hugo's capacious vision of humanity has no room for cynicism: his embrace of the human condition spans centuries and nationalities to speak to something ongoing in the collective temperament. The musical, like Hugo's novel before it, does really and truly hear the people, and who amongst us anywhere in the world doesn't hope that they will be listened to and understood?

It seems appropriate to leave a final word to Mackintosh, who understands this musical to the very essence of his being: "The show is acting like the original novel, in that people wherever they may be don't see this as a foreign show; they see it as their story because human nature is the same the world over: people are fighting for their beliefs in every country in the world."

The happy result is that you simply can't legislate, either in art or in life, for a pull that is quite so primal. One day more? Easily, and the day after that as well. For *Les Misérables* Tomorrow Will Always Come...

Above: *Les Misérables* Dubai opening night card to the cast from Cameron Mackintosh.

Right: Opening night ticket for the Dubai premiere of *Les Misérables*, 15 November 2016.

Opposite, above: "The Prologue". Ensemble of the *Les Misérables* Korean company, 2013.

Opposite, below: "Beggars at the Feast". Im Choon-Gil as Thénardier and Park Joon-Myun as Mme Thénardier with the ensemble, Korea, 2013.

Background: Design by Matt Kinley for the Ballroom in the Wedding scene.

Credits

Authors' Acknowledgements

I would like to thank the following people for giving interviews that provided me with much added insight into the theatrical world of *Les Misérables*. Without their significant input this book would not have been possible: Roger Allam, Alun Armstrong, Michael Ball, Alain Boublil, Susan Boyle, Alistair Brammer, Stephen Brooker, Andrew Bruce, Rebecca Caine, John Caird, Laurence Connor, Dudu Fisher, Freddie Gershon, James Gillingham, Maoko Imai, Richard Jay-Alexander, Matt Kinley, Herbert Kretzmer, Patti LuPone, Terrence Mann, Stephen Metcalfe, Trevor Nunn, James Powell, Philip Quast, Geronimo Rauch, John Robertson, Claude-Michel Schönberg, Jennifer Till, Rachel Vanstone, Alan Wasser and Colm Wilkinson.

I would particularly like to thank Cameron Mackintosh for his huge enthusiasm and fund of stories. The knowledge that both he and Nick Allott brought to the project helped me enormously in the writing of the show's history.

Benedict Nightingale, October 2012

I would like to thank the following people for giving interviews: Samantha Barks, Russell Crowe, Eric Fellner, Anne Hathaway, Debra Hayward, Tom Hooper, Hugh Jackman, Eddie Redmayne, Amanda Seyfried and Aaron Tveit. Many thanks must also go to Stacy Mann, the unit publicist on *Les Misérables*, for arranging set visits, interviews with key cast and crew and miraculously knowing the answers to endless *Les Mis* related questions. Her kindness, supreme professionalism and hard work is much appreciated.

Martyn Palmer, October 2012

I would like to thank Cameron Mackintosh for making the approach in the first place alongside his remarkable team headed by his tireless, encyclopedic and ever good-natured archivist Rosy Runciman and expert designer Thomas Mann. Many thanks, too, to Laurence Connor, Matt Kinley, and Paule Constable for making themselves so brilliantly available at such short notice.

Matt Wolf, May 2018

We are also indebted to Jane Austin, Michael Borowski, Francesca Budd, Jenny Cartwright, Cindy Chang, Chau Digital, Alex Collinson, Natasha Dennison, Dewynters, David Dolman, Rachael Gough, Simon Hayes, Richard Knibb, Katie McMahon, Shidan Majidi, Jen Mitchell, Thomas Schonberg, Sheeraz Shah, Adrian Smith, Ange Teo, Emma Williams and Kate Wyhowska for their invaluable help with the compilation of this volume.

Picture credits

The publishers would like to thank the following sources for their kind permission to reproduce the pictures in this book.

Special thanks are due to Michael Le Poer Trench, who as well as photographing many of the worldwide productions has also captured the behind-the-scenes creation of the show from its inception.

Key: t = Top, b = Bottom, c = Centre,
l = Left and r = Right

Akg Images:
Visioars: 16
The Bridgeman Art Library: / Maison de Victor Hugo, Paris, France / Giraudon: 9b, 17b
© Barbican Centre: 33br
Andrew Bruce: 13

© CML
Photo: Alberto Arzoz: 77
Photo Catherine Ashmore: 6, 53tl, 89, 91, 135t
Photo: Mark Bryan-Brown: 43tl
Photo Matthew Crockett: 44, 141tl, 141b
Photo David Crosswaite: 32t
Photo Michael Le Poer Trench: 8, 10, 21b, 22l, 23, 25-31, 34tr, 34b, 36, 37tl, 40-41, 42c, 42l, 43b, 46-47, 48tc, 48tl, 49-51, 53r, 54r, 55t, 56tl, 56bl, 61l, 61cr, 63tl, 64-65, 68tl, 68tr, 69tl, 70tr, 85t, 88c, 92tl, 95bl, 95br, 108, 131t, 136bl, Back Cover
Photo Joan Marcus: 45bl, 54l, 57, 63tc, 63tr,
Photo Bob Marshak: 21tl
Photo Deen Van Meer: 45br
Photo Alastair Muir: 66r
Photo: Matthew Murphy: 56r, 60, 69tr, 134br, 135b, 138tl, 139t, 139b
Photo Johan Persson: 48tr, 52, 53bl, 55b
Photo Steam Motion and Sound UK: 48b, 86-87
Storyboard: 62
Tony® Award: 58
Photo Unknown: 20, 37bl, 45t, 59, 67t, 75b

CML Archive: 18b
© CMOL: 8, 21tr, 74tr
Design by AKA America: 61tr
Design by AKA Australia: 138bl
Design by Dewynters: Front cover, Front & back endpapers, Title page, 9t, 22c, 22r, 33tl, 33tr, 33bl, 59tl, 76tr, 78, 79l, 84l, 85tr, 85cl, 92bc, 93, 134t, 141cl, 141tr, 141cr, 142tl

Photo © John Carroll: 72tr
Photo © Alan Davidson: 76b
Photo © Phil Dias for Karma Creative: 79r
Photo © DPA Microphones: 119tr
© Dubai Opera: 142bl
Nicholas Garland/*The Daily Telegraph*: 81r
Getty Images: 82t, 85cl
Tim Graham: 35t
Hulton Archive: 11tl
John Phillips: 81t
Time & Life Pictures: 18t
Guinness World Records™: 69cl
Matt Kinley: 90, 92, 135, 137, 139, 140-141, 143
Design by Islawomir Kitowski: 68cr
Herbert Kretzmer/© Shubert Organization, New York: 59tr
Photo Frank Micelotta, Time Magazine: 24
***Les Misérables* Korea Co Ltd.:** 42r, 70cr, 137t, 143t, 143b, 144br
Photo Brian Moody: 32b
Morten Morland/*The Times*: 81l
My Theatre Mates.com: 141tr
John Napier: 33
Andreane Neofitou: 4-5, 12, 35b, 37r
Pimlico Opera: 83
Photo Platon: 140
Private Collection: 11r, 11bl, 17t, 19l
© RMN: /Grand Palais (Musée d'Orsay) / Hervé Lewandowski: 19r
Rex Features: 132, 133t, /Ken McKay: 80r
Photo Jeff Rowley: 123t
Shanghai Grand Theatre: 71r
Photo © Stadsschouwburg Theater, Antwerp: 66l
State Library of Victoria: 138bl
Photo © Theater des Westens, Berlin: 67b
© TOHO CO., LTD. Theatrical Division: 43tr, 45cl, 70tl, 70b, 92bl, 136tl
Photo © Phil Tragen: 115b

© 2012 Universal Studios Licensing LLC. *Les Misérables* movie © Universal Studios. All rights reserved: 9c, 82tf, 94, 95t, 96-103, 105-107, 109-110, 111l, 112-114, 115t, 116-118, 119tl, 119tc, 119b, 120, 122l, 123b, 124-126, 127b, 128-130, 131b, 133br
Eve Stewart: 104, 111r, 121, 122r, 127tr

Photographer unknown: 14, 39, 80cr
Photo © J Willebrand: 67c
Photo © Dan Wooller: 85cr

Every effort has been made to acknowledge correctly and contact the source and/or copyright holder of each picture and Carlton books Ltd apologises for any unintentional errors or omissions, which will be corrected in future editions of the book.

Lyric Credits
Page 127tl: From the movie of *Les Misérables*. Music and Lyrics by Claude-Michel Schönberg, Herbert Kretzmer and Alain Boublil. By kind permission of Alain Boublil Music Limited – Copyright © 2012.

THIS IS A CARLTON BOOK

1990
MIZ AMERICA
MIZ MOOMBA 1990